For my daughter and my father

CONTENTS

I: BIOPHYSICALLY REDUCTIONISTIC PERSONALITY THEORIZING

II: COGNITIVE-AGENTIC AND EGO-PSYCHOLOGICAL PERSONALITY THEORIZING

III: INTERPERSONAL PERSONALITY THEORIZING

Profiles of Personality

~

An Approach-Based Companion

Eugene M. DeRobertis

IV: NESTED INTERPERSONAL
PERSONALITY THEORIZING

Acknowledgments

I would like to thank my wife Heather for her assistance and support throughout the process of writing and editing this book. I would also like to thank my colleague David Stout for reading over this manuscript. Cover art by Violet Void: www.TruePoison.com.

Preface

This book was designed to help me communicate *meaningfully* with my students about personality. It is hoped that the book will prevent students from looking upon personality as "just another psychological concept" they heard about in college. Instead, I wish for students to be able to experience the study of personality as a way of thinking about the dynamic processes of living and lifelong becoming. Accordingly, the text is not arranged chronologically, nor is it structured according to historical lineage. Rather, the theories are presented according to the *kind of approach* that the theorists have taken in order to conceptualize personality. Each approach presents but a "profile" of personality. I find this to be a more effective means for giving students a synoptic grasp of personality and personal growth than relying on time periods or historical affiliations. One need only consider the cases of Freud and Adler to understand my rationale. Freud and Adler were historical contemporaries who worked together and who now share a common lineage (i.e., "psychoanalysis"). However, they produced radically different approaches to personality. Freud is seen by many as a champion of the disavowed "basement" realms of personality, while Adler provided psychologists with a template for a very humanistic, progressive form of interpersonal psychology.

The fact is, there is a range or continuum of perspectives on personality, from the very impersonal, anonymous, atomistic, mechanistic, and reductionistic to the highly interpersonal, meaning-laden, holistic, narrative, and creative. This diversity of viewpoints stands to reason, as human existence is itself so multifaceted. The organization of this book is a reflection of the above noted continuum. It is not the only possible way to express this continuum. It simply happens to be one that I have found productive in facilitating an effective student-teacher dialogue.

This book's structure is indicative of my own views in the sense that I tend to think holistically and dynamically about psychological issues. For this I make no apology. I am simply owning or taking responsibility for my interpretive stance. The purpose of this book is to help students develop a meaningful and coherent sense of personality through the aid of select personality theories. The aim is *not* to blindly conform to the norm of personality textbook construction.

Before proceeding, the reader will note that I have not included citations in the text. Instead, I have included suggested readings at the close of each portion of the book. Since citations interrupt the flow of the material, I have elected to leave them out. This does not mean that I have sacrificed accuracy or academic rigor. I am confident that the reader will see this to be evident in the pages that follow. Moreover, I have not included biographical material on the theorists presented here. This is not intended to minimize the importance of biographical data. Rather, my intent was to stay focused on how each approach illuminates significant aspects of personality. As a *companion*, this book is not intended to be a substitute for a detailed introductory textbook or for primary source material from the personality theorists themselves.

CHAPTER 1
Brief Introduction

Like so many topics in psychology (e.g., intelligence, emotion, motivation, health, psychopathology, etc.), *personality* lacks a universally agreed upon conceptualization. Instead, what one finds is a diversity of viewpoints on the topic, each with its own manner of interpreting what personality is and how it forms. In fact, few personality theorists have taken the time to formally define personality. A notable exception to this general trend is Gordon Allport who defined personality as *the dynamic organization within the individual of those psychophysical systems that determine her characteristic behavior and thought.* This is perhaps the best definition of personality to date. Stated in simpler terms, when psychologists use the term "personality," it is meant to refer to *the relatively stable pattern or style of behavior that gives an organism its individuality.*

Personality psychologists attempt to understand how human beings achieve a degree of integrated functioning in life, which is a fact that often goes unnoticed on a day-to-day basis. It is only when a person's behavior appears "erratic" or "conflicted" that we seem to notice what we all take for granted: the typically *organized* nature of human living. This organization has a consistency that allows one to confidently describe a human being's personality to others. If human beings acted in radically divergent ways from moment-to-moment, day-to-day, it would be impossible to describe your friend Kim as "easy-going," for example. This does not mean that Kim must *always* be easy-going. We understand implicitly that personality refers to a *typical* manner of behaving for which there can be exceptions. Personality is a very broad term in this way.

In addition to being relatively consistent, personality has an individualized quality about it. If all human beings were to act in the exact same manner, there would be no reason to speak about or study personality. The study of personality would simply be the study of human behavior, nothing more. If all human beings were easy-going, then your description of your friend Kim as easy-going would be a superfluous statement of the obvious. The concept of personality bears with it the assumption that human beings achieve a degree of integrated, relatively consistent functioning that is particular to each individual. It is the job of personality theories to make sense out of data pertaining to the achievement of this individualized consistency.

Theories of personality are, at a minimum, scientific tools that have at least two purposes. On the one hand, theories of personality are used to organize and make sense out of research findings pertaining to personality. Psychology is not a "purely" empirical or "strictly" observation-based discipline. Theory is involved every step of the way. The results of empirical observations are sometimes the subject of intense theoretical debate, and the results of studies are often reinterpreted over time as theoretical viewpoints in psychology come in and out of vogue. At one point in history, findings are the result of a learning process. At another point, the very same findings are attributable to brain anomalies. On the other hand, theories are used to generate and guide research. When theoretical viewpoints clash, it stimulates a new set of studies designed to explore this new conceptual avenue. Even the research tactics employed in these studies will have theoretical grounding.

A psychological theory is a set of assumptions that research can in some way or other support or contest. If *no* observations can be used to make an argument in favor or against a theory of personality, it probably does not qualify as psychological in nature. Stated differently, if the so-called theory is *purely* faith-based, then it no longer falls squarely within the realm of *scientific* psychological inquiry. However, this does not mean that theories can be proven or disproven wholesale. Theories are large, broad-based narratives, and no single study or group of studies can validate or invalidate an entire theory. Rather, the viability of parts or aspects of a theory can be examined through research. In this way, a theory is distinguished from say, a hypothesis, which is small enough to be tested.

Good theories have certain characteristics that all students of personality should know. For example, a good theory is philosophically consistent. That is, a theory should not violate the law of non-contradiction. If a theory consists of truth claims that simply contradict one another, then the theory will be judged as weak. This is not to say that there cannot be opposing truth claims within a theory at all. A theory can make opposing claims, so long as the theorist demonstrates an awareness of this opposition and provides explanations for the *seeming* contradiction. Indeed, human existence is very complex, and a theory that lacks such irregularities altogether might be accused of being too linear and myopic. Sometimes behavior can appear radically different under different circumstances, as a matter of course.

Another characteristic of a good theory is an awareness of historical, social, and cultural context. All theories throughout all of the sciences are created from within a time and place in history. Good personality theorizing is cognizant of the fact that the context out of which a theory arises can have an effect on the final form of the theory. Without such awareness, the theory can be accused of being biased in some way (e.g., as being ethnocentric, androcentric, and so forth).

Yet another aspect of good theorizing is that it avoids the opposing extremes of obfuscation and oversimplification. *In the absence of compelling evidence to the contrary*, the simplest explanation for behavior is the best explanation for behavior. The simplest explanation is not always the best explanation by a long shot. However, it is best not to complexify something that is in fact quite simple. At the same time, one must avoid the temptation to lunge at linear, skeletal, or superficial explanations for phenomena that have depth and subtlety to them. Good personality theorizing helps psychologists navigate between very simple and very complex behavioral dynamics. This is an important point, as the ability to efficiently understand the nature of one's observations empowers psychologists to make reasonable decisions with regard to therapeutic interventions, pedagogical interventions, and various public and institutional policies.

Finally, good theorizing is cognizant of the value of empirical observation. That is, it values support from *both* quantitative and qualitative research. This should not be mistaken for a naive advocacy of "data-driven" *methodologism*. This would contradict the aforementioned remarks concerning the role of theory in the study of personality. The fact is that all research, quantitative and qualitative, is ultimately open-ended in nature. There is always more to learn, more to discover, more to reveal, more to explicate, more to articulate, more to explain, and more to understand. Theorizing both frames the parameters of research and allows us to think beyond the scope of the "hard data" before us. Thus, there is currently a largely unheard cry for theory in psychology to save it from the ravages of a myopic focus on methodology. Theoretical psychology has recently emerged as a subdiscipline all its own for just these reasons.

Psychologists are in search of theoretical guidance that allows for analysis at manifold levels of human functioning, from the very simple to the infinitely complex. This search for theoretical guidance is pervasive and can be observed in the area of research methodology itself. Research psychologists are demonstrating an ever-increasing need for theoretical frameworks that can capture the subtleties of the data they collect. While qualitative research psychologists have long known about the need for such frameworks, quantitative research is now following suit as it slowly shifts its emphasis from null hypothesis significance testing to a modeling orientation. This is a *theoretical* shift from proposing that a hypothesis has merit by rejecting the probability that one's research results were random to constructing models that accurately portray multifaceted human interactions. Psychology cannot avoid theory. Personality theories are invaluable tools of the psychologist's trade.

Suggested Readings

DeRobertis, E. M. (2012). *The whole child: Selected papers on existential-humanistic child psychology*. Charleston, SC: CreateSpace Publishing.

Kuhn, T. (1996). *The structure of scientific revolutions*. Chicago: University Of Chicago Press.

Slife, B. (2000). Division presidential address: The practice of theoretical psychology. *Journal of Theoretical and Philosophical Psychology, 20*, 97-115.

I: BIOPHYSICALLY REDUCTIONISTIC PERSONALITY THEORIZING

CHAPTER 2
Personality as a
Reflection of Inherited Traits

At the present time, psychologists on a mass scale are enamored with the biological aspects of human living. There are many factors responsible for bringing about this turn of events, such as the numerous technological advances that have enabled scientists to probe the brain and the human genome. Thus, it should come as no surprise to find that there are psychologists who have suggested that personality can be looked upon as a genetically inherited phenomenon. In fact, this idea underlies the most popular form of thinking on the topic of personality today, which is the *big five trait theory* most closely affiliated with two individuals, Robert R. McCrae and Paul T. Costa.

The story of trait theory, however, begins with the aforementioned Gordon Allport. Allport observed that individuals tend to display a relatively unique conglomeration of behavioral and experiential characteristics that manifest themselves with a degree of consistency. He called these characteristics *traits* and set out to gather together the various trait descriptors that have been employed by human beings through a study of the English language. Allport poured through unabridged dictionaries and accumulated thousands of trait words. He pondered the idea that it might be possible to study these descriptors and develop relevant insights for personality theorizing. Allport observed that, in the lives of individuals, some traits appear more frequently than others, while some have a stronger motivational influence than others. Overall, his focus tended to come back to the concrete object of psychological science, which is the living, breathing human being.

As it would happen, various psychologists to come along after Allport decided that it is not enough to consider the breadth of human trait descriptors and get a sense of how they cluster *in the lives of individuals*. These psychologists developed an inclination to bundle traits into parcels that they believed would give traits a more trans-individual, universal, or law-like flavor. Psychologists like Raymond Cattell, for instance, initiated a psychometric, *factor analytic* program of research wherein traits were mathematically analyzed in such a way as to reduce many traits down to a set of more "basic" factors (i.e., broad categories or general headings). These basic factors were defined by clusters of trait descriptors that were found to correlate with each another. By using instruments to make inquiries of research participants (e.g., questionnaires, various tests constructed to study personality, etc.), clusters of traits were pulled together and dubbed *factor loadings*.

Cattell first arrived at a list of thirty-five traits, which were then later factor analyzed down to a core of sixteen primary trait categories. It was at the tally of sixteen that Cattell finally felt comfortable (Cattell struggled with the mathematics of his analysis a bit and has been criticized for being mathematically imprecise). These sixteen traits included *abstractedness, apprehension, dominance, emotional stability, liveliness, openness to change, perfectionism, privateness, reasoning, rule consciousness, self-reliance, sensitivity, social boldness, tension, vigilance,* and *warmth.* Each category was comprised of traits that would indicate if a person had more or less of the primary factor in question. So, for instance, scoring low on *warmth* would be described with words like impersonal, distant, cool, reserved, detached, formal, or aloof. However, scoring high on *warmth* would be described with words like warm, outgoing, attentive to others, kindly, easy-going, participating, or likes people. Moreover, and this is vitally important to the current discussion, Raymond Cattell asserted that some traits are probably strongly rooted in genes while others are more likely the result of culture.

This established an important precedent. Soon, another psychologist named Hans Eysenck would come along, develop his own factor analytic depiction of traits, and eventually claim that traits rooted in genetics should have *top priority* in personality research. Eysenck further asserted that the genetic influence on these traits should be readily apparent in the architecture of the brain. Eysenck drew inspiration from the personality theory of Carl Jung in his research. Jung is one of the people responsible for bringing an evolutionary sort of perspective into psychology via psychoanalysis. Thus, Eysenck's basic or primary trait categories have a strong Jungian ring to them and a strong clinical flavor as well. They consist of *extraversion, neuroticism,* and *psychoticism.* As an example of Eysenck's model, the factor loading for *psychoticism* includes aggressive, cold, egocentric, impersonal, impulsive, antisocial, unempathic, creative, and tough-minded.

Today, the previously noted big five theory of Robert McCrae and Paul Costa, has risen to a veritable superstar status, achieving a higher degree of popularity than any other approach to personality. More and more it seems that Cattell and Eysenck are being considered mere precursors to the establishment of the big five model (which neither of them endorsed). The big five research model is comprised of *extraversion, neuroticism, openness to experience, agreeableness,* and *conscientiousness*. Each of these factors has a bipolar nature, such that certain traits descriptors are affiliated with scoring high with regard to the factor in question while opposing descriptors are affiliated with scoring low with regard to the factor in question. So, for instance, high *extraversion* includes descriptors like affectionate, joiner, talkative, fun loving, active, and passionate. Low *extraversion* is comprised of descriptors like reserved, loner, quiet, sober, passive, and unfeeling.

The reader should note that McCrae and Costa created a *research model* (called the five factor model or FFM) and worked diligently to establish that the "correct" number of primary traits is five. They have done an efficient job of promoting the strength of their research, asserting that the final tally of five has been "discovered" and that the pieces of the personality puzzle are "finally" falling in place (in spite of the fact that there is no universal agreement on this point in the field of personality research). McCrae and Costa then designed a *big five theory* of personality (a five factor theory or FFT) *retroactively* or *post hoc*, meaning *after* they established their program of research. In doing so, McCrae and Costa noted that their theory adds little to what has already been contributed by the great personality theorists. A primary reason for this is that McCrae and Costa harkened back to Eysenck's approach and asserted that *personality is primarily a genetic and biological phenomenon*. Personality traits (and thus the essence of personality) are passed along through genes and are embedded in the architecture of the brain. To be sure, McCrae and Costa did carve out a place in their theory for things like adaptations to specific environments, including the development of self-schemas and personal myths. Culture is held to contribute to individual differences in personality, but *personality is genetic and biological (e.g., neurological and hormonal) in origin.* It is inherited, "primary" traits that ultimately account for the deep structure and stability of personality. The big five *theory* basically adopted another, perhaps somewhat more biogenetically adamant version of Eysenck's general approach to personality even though Eysenck did not endorse the big five factor model and would thus not have agreed on what to look for in genes or the brain.

Today, the five-factor *research model* is thrown about without much care for the fact that it is not a theory of personality. The distinction between the research model and the personality theory is often overlooked, blurred, or minimized. In accounting for the relatively unique contours of an individual's personality, the idea is that human beings inherit varying amounts of each big five factor. These inherited quantities accumulate to form the basis of *who* one is. The big five have thus become a master recipe of sorts. Advocates of the approach have even gathered data from samples of people from other cultures to argue that the big five are universal.

Due to these cross-cultural data collection efforts, cultural psychologists are taking the big five concept seriously. At the same time, some researchers have reservations about this research, particularly as regards the extent of its applicability and its thoroughness. For example, Sampo V. Paunonen and his colleagues have noted that the big five theory does not account for a host of traits such as *religious, sly, honest, sexy, thrifty, conservative, masculine-feminine, egotistical, humorous,* and *risk-taking,* which may be better able to account for variations in culturally relevant behaviors in places like Canada, England, Germany, and Finland.

Even more recently, neuroscience has followed suit. Studies have begun to surface claiming to have provided evidence that big five traits are embedded within the architecture of the brain. For example, in a study done by Colin G. DeYoung, Jacob B. Hirsh, Matthew S. Shane, Xenophon Papademetris, Nallakkandi Rajeevan, and Jeremy R. Gray, the authors noted that certain big five traits can be seen to covary with the volume of neural tissue in various parts of the brain. Extraversion covaries with the volume of medial orbitofrontal cortex, which is a brain region involved in processing reward information. Neuroticism covaries with the volume of brain regions associated with threat, punishment, and negative affect.

Agreeableness covaries with the volume of neural tissue in areas that process information about the intentions and mental states of other individuals. Finally, conscientiousness covaries with the volume of brain tissue in the lateral prefrontal cortex, a region involved in planning and the voluntary control of behavior. However, openness to experience was *not* found to covary with the volume of neural tissue in any significant way (in general, openness is perhaps the most problematic trait to "locate" neurologically). This discrepancy has led Colin DeYoung to hypothesize that there might really be only *two* essential personality indicators, one being *stability* (comprised of what the big five theory would call agreeableness, conscientiousness, and neuroticism) and the other being *plasticity* (comprised of what the big five theory would call extraversion and openness to experience).

In the area of genetics, a variant of what has been termed the *5-HTTLPR gene* (a serotonin-transporter-linked polymorphic region gene) has been linked to the trait of *neuroticism*. However, the effects of this allele are small and cannot be replicated consistently, much less universally. These studies serve to demonstrate both the enthusiasm and the hesitations that the big five approach has evoked among social scientists. The fact is that genes interact both with each other and environments in ways that are extremely complex and sometimes unpredictable. Thus, a discrete, unambiguous link between genes, brain structures, and resultant traits (at least of the kind being discussed here) will likely be difficult to come by.

Interestingly, evolutionary psychology, which is grounded in genetic and biological theorizing by way of its emphasis on natural selection, does not always square with big five theory. For example, David Buss, a leading authority in evolutionary psychology and trait research from an evolutionary perspective, has noted that personality has moderate heritability at best (i.e., thirty to fifty percent). Moreover, whereas trait theory views its traits as relatively context-free, evolutionary approaches tend to look upon inherited dispositions as situation specific adaptations, beneficial tendencies adopted as a solution to a certain environmental stumbling blocks. So, for example, humans are far more apt to fear creatures like spiders or snakes (which can kill you) than other animals. Cognitive scientist Jerry Fodor has dubbed niche-oriented dispositions that occur very consistently among the members of a species *modules*.

David Buss and his colleague Kenneth Craik are sympathetic to the trait approach (even in its factor analytic forms), noting that the identification of central trait concepts from among thousands remains a vital theoretical task for personality psychology. However, Buss and Craik have never restricted their thinking to big five traits. Buss and Craik have employed an *act frequency approach* to derive traits (sometimes called *dispositions*). Dispositions are considered summaries of act frequencies. Act frequencies are conceptual units that summarize general trends in conduct. Far from being purely or even mainly genetic, dispositions are *sociocultural emergents* that function as "natural" cognitive classifications for actions. Buss and Craik's version of evolutionary theory (and there are several versions) *rejects* the nature-nurture distinction. Using this approach, Buss and Craik have identified what they consider to be some important ingredients in the processes inherent to personality formation, including *quarrelsome, agreeable, dominant, submissive, gregarious*, and *aloof.* For Buss and Craik, these category boundaries are not sharply demarcated. They blend into one another and the actions associated with each category can vary widely.

Moreover, Buss and Craik are explicit about the fact that these traits are merely descriptive, not etiological, and thus *explain nothing about the personality as a whole.* In spite of its admirable contributions to psychological knowledge, it is not easy for evolutionary theory to directly address the issue of personality because it is not fully equipped as yet to answer questions that deviate too far from species-typical explanatory principles. Evolutionary psychology places emphasis on *species-typical mechanisms* such as niche picking or strategic specialization, adaptive decision rules, and self-serving mating strategies. For example, in Buss's view, an evolutionary viewpoint implies that males and females should differ in terms of what makes them jealous in relationships. Males ought to be more jealous regarding the potential for sexual infidelity in a mate, which would lessen their ability to pass along their genetic material. Females, on the other hand, should become more jealous over the threat of losing resources if they should lose their mates. These are *hypothesized general trends* whose applicability to individual lives embedded in their unique contexts is still quite open to question. As Buss has noted, variations from the species behavioral norm have long been considered *genetic junk* or *noise* that is unrelated to the core of the evolutionary process. This is not to say that individual differences have no role at all in evolutionary thought. Diversity adds to the flexibility of a species to fit into varying environmental niches. Nonetheless, the overall thrust of evolutionary thought is the species rather than the individual.

Final Remarks

This chapter considered the idea of looking upon personality as an aggregate of inherited traits, with varying degrees of each trait accounting for individuality. There are many trait theories advocating for different dispositional constellations, but not all of them are so genetically oriented. The most genetically oriented happens to be the most popular, which is the big five theory. This theory proposes that individual differences are best understood on the basis of *extraversion, neuroticism, openness to experience, agreeableness,* and *conscientiousness,* each of which is held to be the product of inheritance.

To reiterate, the mathematical process of reducing thousands of culturally embedded trait descriptors down to the thirty-five, twenty-two, twenty, sixteen, nine, five, three, or two (there have been many tallies) that most convincingly allow one to probabilistically account for variations in behavior on a mass scale does not in and of itself constitute a personality theory. The conflation of research model and theory that has permeated the discipline of psychology on the whole reflects a form of bias in contemporary psychology in favor of viewpoints that are *atomistic* in nature and prone to oversimplification. Atomistic psychology takes complex structure and reduces it down to its minimally workable elements or lowest common denominator. For this reason, it is sometimes referred to as *reductionistic*.

In spite of its popularity, not all psychologists are convinced that the big five approach is optimal for understanding personality, even those sympathetic to the notion of a trait theory. For example, Dan McAdams and Jennifer Pals have recently noted that personality researchers ought move beyond their preoccupation with "the" big five traits as discrete entities and develop a truly *integrative* vision of the whole person as a unique individual. They proposed simply conceptualizing personality as an individual's unique variation on the general evolutionary design for human nature, expressed as a developing pattern of dispositional traits, characteristic adaptations, and self-defining life narratives complexly and differentially embedded in a cultural and social context. The notion of evolutionary remnants emerging within the lives of individuals through the medium of culture-specific forms of expression will be revisited in the chapter on Carl Jung. For now, it is time to turn up the microscope and get into the dirty details of how people interact with their environments.

Suggested Readings

Allport, G. W. (1968). *The person in psychology: Selected essays.* Boston: Beacon Press.

Buss, D. M. & Craik, K. H. (1981). The act frequency analysis of interpersonal dispositions: Aloofness, gregariousness, dominance and submissiveness. *Journal of Personality, 49,* 175-192.

Cattell, R. B. (2007). *The scientific analysis of personality.* Piscataway, NJ: Aldine Transaction.

DeYoung, C. G. Hirsh, J. B., Shane, M. S., Papademetris, X., Rajeevan, N., & Gray, J. R. (2012). Testing predictions from personality neuroscience: Brain structure and the big five. *Psychological Science,* 21, 820-828.

Eysenck, H. J. & Eysenck, S. B. G. (2006). *The biological basis of personality.* Piscataway, NJ: Aldine Transaction

Fodor, J. A. (1983). *The modularity of mind: An essay on faculty psychology.* Cambridge: MIT.

McAdams, D. P. & Pals, J. L. (2006). A new big five: Fundamental principles for an integrative science of personality. *American Psychologist, 61,* 204-217.

McCrae, R. R. & Costa, P. T. (2003). *Personality in adulthood, second edition: A five-factor theory perspective.* New York: Guilford.

Paunonen, S. V. & Jackson, D. N. (2000). What is beyond the big five? Plenty! *Journal of Personality, 68,* 821-835.

Smits, D. J. M. & Boeck, P. D. (2006). From BIS/BAS to the Big Five. *European Journal of Personality, 20,* 255-270.

CHAPTER 3
Watson and Skinner: Personality as an Aggregate of Conditioned Responses

In this chapter, we will look at approaches to personality that look to the *environment* for the causes of personality formation. Although these approaches do acknowledge that personality formation occurs within genetic parameters, they emphatically reject the use of internal (i.e., mental) states as a *primary* means for explaining behavior or personality. Rather, behavior and personality are considered the result of repeated exposure to specific environmental *conditions*. Hence, these theories are called *conditioning theories*. They come from the school of thought known as *behaviorism*. From this vantage point, if one were to inquire as to the origin of certain patterns of behavior, one should not look "inward" to the individual's thoughts, beliefs, values, and so forth. Rather, one ought to look outward for the causes of behavior in the individual's "readily observable" environmental conditions. Thus, conditioning theory does not consider how much things like your mother, your home, or your dog might *mean* to you to be valid environmental data. For a strict behaviorist, the *meaning* of your environmental interactions is far too mental or "intrapsychic" to be given focal consideration. Conditioning theories take the very strict position that anything that is to be considered truly "scientific" must be measurable, and environmental interactions that cannot be measured are thus deemed inherently problematic.

Classical Conditioning Theory

The first behavioral learning theory to appear in the history of psychology was classical conditioning theory. The story of classical conditioning theory is rooted in the work of the Russian physiologist Ivan Pavlov. Pavlov was studying the reflexive (i.e., involuntary) responses involved in the digestion of food. In order to study digestion, Pavlov studied dogs. In order to study their digestive processes, Pavlov had to feed his dogs. Over time, Pavlov came to notice that his dogs were salivating *before* he presented them with food. This was strange to Pavlov. As a physiologist, he knew that the involuntary response of salivation was naturally elicited by the sight, smell, or taste of food. What he saw, however, was that the response of salivation could be elicited without seeing, smelling, or tasting any food. This was not natural, therefore it must have been *learned*.

Pavlov hypothesized that the dogs were salivating before they perceived food because a simple form of learning had taken place called *associative learning*. He ventured that an *association* had occurred, a linking or joining of the appearance of the person delivering the food with the food itself. Each stimulus became an indicator of the other. What has now become known as *classical conditioning* is the process by which the "systematic pairing" of stimuli creates associative links. As a result of such links, any response brought on by one of the stimuli would spread, so to speak, so that the organism in question would come to elicit the same response to the new (previously "neutral") stimulus.

To test this, Pavlov surgically implanted tubes into his dogs' salivary glands so that he could measure the amount of saliva that they produced. He was able to compare how much saliva was in a dog's mouth at any given time as opposed to how much saliva would be produced when presented with food. Pavlov then searched for something that would act as a neutral stimulus. That is, he searched for something that would not elicit any more salivation than usual in the dogs' mouths. His choice for a neutral stimulus was a bell. Pavlov rang a bell and noticed that the dogs did not salivate any more than usual when they heard it. At this point, Pavlov began systematically pairing the ringing of the bell with the presentation of food. Over and over again, the bell would ring before feeding time. Eventually, Pavlov was able to demonstrate that after systematically pairing the ringing of the bell with the presentation of food, he could get the dogs to salivate to the sound of the bell similar to the way they would salivate to the presentation of food *even in the absence of any food perception*. In other words, the dogs would produce copious amounts of saliva when they heard the bell, even though they were not seeing, smelling, or tasting any food. This, for Pavlov, was evidence in favor of his ideas concerning associative learning.

Pavlov gave names to the variables in his study. The food was called the *unconditioned stimulus*. In simpler language, this means that the food was the "not taught" stimulation. One does not have to teach dogs about food. They have a preexisting response to it, which is salivation. The salivation to the food was thus called the *unconditioned response*. The bell, in contrast, was dubbed the *conditioned stimulus*. Dogs do not naturally salivate when bells ring, so the bell was thus the *taught* or *learned* stimulation. The dogs learned to salivate to the sound of the bell. Their salivation to the bell was dubbed the *conditioned response*. The conditioned response is the brand new reaction of the organism. It is the new learned behavior and the evidence that classical conditioning has taken place.

Pavlov won the Nobel Prize in physiology for his work. His field, recall, was *not* psychology. However, in the United States, the up-and-coming psychologist John Watson saw in Pavlov's physiology the fulfillment of a new form of psychology that he was developing called *behaviorism*. For Watson, the principles of conditioning furnished a way of doing psychology that was precise and unhampered by concepts that he found vague and troublesome, like mind, consciousness, introspection, and so forth. Watson sought a "purely objective" (ideally, experimental) psychology that would be a proper representative of the natural sciences. The goal of this psychology would be prediction and the control of behavior. Accordingly, he went to work straightaway at carrying out studies that would import conditioning theory into the psychology of human beings.

In one of his more controversial studies, he and his associate Rosalie Rayner secured the "participation" of an eight-month-old baby boy who was given the pseudonym "Little Albert." The aim of their study was to condition Albert to have an emotional reaction of fear. They would thereby demonstrate that the kinds of procedures at play in Pavlov's experiments were also operative in determining the behavior of human beings. Watson and Rayner found that if they struck a suspended steel bar with a hammer they could frighten Little Albert. They then proceeded to expose Little Albert to a white (laboratory) rat and noted that Albert showed *no* apprehension with regard to this stimulus. That is, he was *not* afraid of the rat. They then systematically paired the presentation of the rat with the loud, sharp sound of a hammer hitting a steel bar. Over and over again, when Little Albert would encounter the rat, he was made afraid by the unsettling sound of a hammer hitting a steel bar. Over time, simply presenting the rat alone to Albert caused him alarm. Little Albert did not fear rats at first. But after the successive presentation of the rat with the fear-evoking stimulus of a clanging metal bar, Albert came to fear the laboratory rat. Through this systematic pairing, Little Albert was classically conditioned to elicit an emotional reaction of fear.

The kinds of studies done by Watson and other early behaviorists were believed to have important implications for a theory of human behavior that could be transferred over into the study of personality. From this perspective, our relatively consistent behavioral patterns would be seen as a mere aggregate of conditioned responses, like those in Pavlov's and Watson's studies. Consider the following behavioral discrepancy: one young lady is quite fond of school while her friend is apprehensive about school and dislikes it. To shed light on these personal differences one would consider their histories of associations with school. From this perspective, what we might expect to find is a process similar to what occurred in the case of Little Albert. Perhaps the first young lady repeatedly had fun in school, had a teacher who liked her, found it easy to get help, and found school to be a generally pleasant place. These pleasurable associations would lead us to predict that she *should* be fond of school. Perhaps her friend was teased, perhaps she had negative interactions with her teacher, or maybe she had a difficult time with her studies. From these aversive associations we would predict that she should indeed dislike school. The point is, we would not look primarily inward to their mental states to explain this kind of difference in personal style. Instead, we would focus our attention on their environments for clues as to the history of their associations with school. It is here that one would find the "objective" evidence or *cause* of their respective dispositions toward school.

At this point, you might be asking yourself, can all of human behavior really be explained in such simple terms? After all, there is a lot of diversity in human behavior. This is a valid point, and the behaviorists have not overlooked this fact. Watson himself contributed to the behaviorist's response to this query. When Watson and Rayner conditioned Little Albert to fear a rat, they soon noticed that his conditioned response of fear was not limited to the conditioned stimulus (i.e., the rat). They reported that his fear reaction generalized beyond the rat to all sorts of stimuli that were vaguely similar to the rat, such as a dog, a rabbit, a fur coat, and a white bearded Santa Claus mask. This phenomenon was dubbed *stimulus generalization*, and it is used as a way of explaining how human beings develop so many diverse and strange behavioral patterns. Given the way new learned responses can spread far and wide to all kinds of related stimuli, it thus makes sense that we should see diversity in human behavior.

Consider the development of phobias as an example. There are a great many phobias among the general population, and some of them are bizarre. For example, I was once acquainted with a young lady who was phobic of pasta! Now, being afraid of something like a dog or a snake seems understandable to people. All it would take would be an instance of being bitten, or at least seeing someone bitten. But how could we explain a pasta phobia? She had never been hurt by pasta or even injured in the presence of pasta. It turned out that this young lady associated pasta with maggots, which were associated with rot and death. As she probed into the source of the behavior, she began to unearth a series of associations, which led to maggots. Now, many forms of pasta could be seen as sort of worm-like in appearance (e.g., spaghetti). Thus, a behaviorist could explain her phobia by searching for the initial environmental interactions or learning experiences from whence she first became afraid in the presence of maggots and thereby generalized her fear response.

Here you might object, "But not *all* learned responses generalize!" This is also true, and behaviorists have a way to explain that as well. It is called *discrimination learning*. Sometimes organisms come to elicit conditioned responses to a specific stimulus apart from all others. The organism can learn to discriminate the stimulus by unambiguous properties or traits, like training a dolphin to take hostile action against predatory sharks rather than docile sharks to protect divers. An interesting instance of discriminatory learning is the *Garcia Effect* or *conditioned taste aversion*. When an organism experiences nausea or vomits, it is not unusual for that organism to avoid that *particular* food or drink in the future. Other forms of food or drink are unaffected.

So classical conditioning theorists hypothesized that all learning and thus, personality formation, takes place this way. It proceeds from basic associations to more complicated and varied associations, which facilitates *higher-order conditioning*. This is the process by which an organism forms new associations through exposure to a previously conditioned (i.e., learned) stimulus. So, for example, Pavlov's dogs were conditioned to salivate to the sound of a bell. From here, one could then expose the dogs to the color green each time the bell rings and we might eventually see the dogs salivate to the color green.

Before moving on, it must be noted that this kind of learning does not have to be permanent. Behaviorists have noted that if the particular kind of pairing in question (i.e., the particular environmental exposure) is stopped, then over time new learned responses can go extinct. *Extinction* refers to the phenomenon where a learned behavior stops occurring due to the elimination or alteration of the environmental conditions that were responsible for the appearance of that behavior in the first place. However, this is not to say that extinction is a given either. In fact, sometimes a response that has gone extinct can suddenly reemerge for a brief period. This is called *spontaneous recovery*, though such responses are rarely as powerful as the initial learned response.

Operant Conditioning Theory

Operant conditioning theory is the second major viewpoint to appear in the behavioral tradition and it expands the basic ideas of classical conditioning theory. In agreement with classical conditioning theorists, operant conditioning theorists consider human personality to be the result of environmental conditions, which give rise to associations that come to elicit new learned behaviors. However, operant conditioning theory will be less about the generic pairing of stimuli and more about associations tied to *the consequences* of an organism's *actions*, as we will see momentarily.

Operant conditioning was first termed *instrumental learning* by Edward L. Thorndike. Thorndike paved the way for this new development in behaviorism. Thorndike studied the behavior of cats trying to escape from puzzle boxes. At first, it took the cats a long time to escape. Over time, however, incorrect solutions were phased out and successful responses occurred more frequently. This pruning and honing of responses allowed the cats to escape faster with practice. With his *law of effect*, Thorndike theorized that responses that produce *satisfying* consequences become forged in memory, which makes them occur more frequently over time. In contrast, unsuccessful responses (which produce frustrating consequences), are discarded and thus occur less frequently. In other words, rewarding consequences *strengthen* a behavior and frustrating consequences *weaken a* behavior.

B. F. Skinner later called this form of learning *operant conditioning* because he felt it was more descriptive. For Skinner, organisms operate on things in the world. An *operant* is thus a method that can be used to modify behavioral interactions over time. These operations have consequences that will have a direct impact on future behavior or future "operations," as it were. According to the principles of Skinnerian conditioning, an action can be strengthened or suppressed depending upon whether the organism receives reinforcements (i.e., rewards) or punishments *after* performing the behavior. If an organism carries out an action and, as a consequence, receives a reinforcement, the behavior that preceded the reinforcement will be more likely to occur again. If an organism carries out an action and, as a consequence, receives a punishment, the behavior that preceded the punishment will be less likely to occur again. In other words, a reinforcer is any event that increases the probability of a behavior reoccurring. A punisher is any event that decreases the probability of a behavior reoccurring.

Skinner noted that there are different forms of reinforcement and punishment. For example, there are *positive* and *negative* reinforcement and punishment. The terms *positive* and *negative* are often troublesome for students learning about operant conditioning because the two terms are typically used to make value judgments in everyday life. However, positive does not mean good and negative does not mean bad. Rather, positive means *add* and negative means *subtract*. Thus, *positive reinforcement* means to reward by way of adding something, such as *giving* praise or *giving* money after a behavior to increase the probability that it will occur again. *Negative reinforcement* means taking something away in order to reward the organism, like removing an unwanted curfew or an unpleasant chore. This is reinforcing because an aversive stimulus has been removed.

In contrast, *positive punishment* refers to the presentation of an aversive stimulus for an undesired behavior. For example, yelling at an organism or hitting it for performing a behavior would likely decrease the probability that the behavior would occur again. *Negative punishment* involves removing something for the purposes of punishing the organism, like taking away a child's allowance or television time.

Skinner also distinguished between primary and secondary reinforcers and punishers. Consequences classified as *primary* relate to the basic biological needs of the organism and have a direct bearing on its survival. In other words, primary reinforcements and punishments do not have to be conditioned or learned. One easy way to think about this class of reinforcers and punishers is to consider neonatal infants who have not been subject to much by way of learning. If an infant would find it rewarding or punishing, it is likely primary. So, for instance, a delicious drink of milk (as a reward) or the prick of a needle (as a punishment) would both belong to the primary class. However, consider the presentation of a hundred dollar bill (as a reward) or the loss of a diamond ring (as a punishment). These consequences would be valueless to an infant. They have great potential to influence the behavior of an adult, however, due to the adult's having learned about their potential for reward through associative learning (e.g., the one hundred dollar bill can buy you a lot of delicious milk). Thus, the latter two examples would be called secondary reinforcement and punishment respectively.

Given what has been said of operant conditioning theory thus far, one can begin to see its ramifications for approaching the problem of human personality. The relatively consistent behavioral responses that would be cited as indicative of a "personality" emerge due to the individual having been reinforced for those behaviors. Behaviors that have not been rewarded or have been punished would thus be less likely to occur and less likely to become part of the personality in question. Thus, personality "types" are created or made not only through repeated exposure to specific environments (as in classical conditioning), but also through the reinforcement and punishment of behavioral responses. If one were to speak of an addictive personality, for example, one would explain its appearance on the basis of the rewarding effects of the drugs that the individual has consumed. With each reinforcement, the behavior that preceded it (i.e., the obtaining and consuming of the drugs) is more likely to occur and become a regular pattern of action. Given enough time, the person will become physically and psychologically adapted to intoxication, such that the absence of the drug will create withdrawal symptoms. Now, consuming the drug will alleviate withdrawal in addition to creating positive sensations. In effect, the process of creating a so-called addictive personality in an otherwise normal individual is the process of compounding positive reinforcement with negative reinforcement.

The gradual process of creating a complex mosaic of behaviors is further comprehensible on the basis of what operant conditioning theorists call *shaping*. Complex patterns of behavior develop over time with many different instances of reinforcement. Any parent knows this well. In order to get one's child to behave in a disciplined, well-structured manner, the parent has to enforce structure through the use of many different reinforcements (and sometimes punishments as well). Shaping refers to the process of reinforcing successive approximations of the desired behavior or behaviors until the organism at last learns the behavioral repertoire being taught. So, for instance, a parent can reward a child with praise for picking up her clothes. Then she can be rewarded *not merely* for picking up her clothes, but *also* for putting her toys away. Eventually, over time, the child will be keeping her entire room neat and tidy so long as the parent can maintain patience and persistence.

A favorite operant conditioning technique of parents is to reinforce in accord with *Premack's Principle*. According to this principle, an organism will perform a less desirable activity to obtain a desirable activity. So, a parent might be able to get a child to clean her room (the less desired activity) if, in doing so, it gains her the reward of being able to go and play with her friends (the more desired activity).

When shaping an organism via the use of reinforcements, one may use different *schedules of reinforcement* to operantly condition an organism. Reinforcements can be distributed according to amounts of time, in which case they are called *interval* schedules. Alternatively, reinforcements can be distributed according to amounts of work, in which case they are called *ratio* schedules. Interval and ratio schedules can be either fixed or variable. A *fixed interval schedule* means that the organism will be rewarded after a fixed time interval, say, every 30 seconds, so long as it is performing the behavior to be rewarded. This schedule causes high response frequency near the end of the interval, but slower responding immediately after the delivery of the reinforcer. A *variable interval schedule* means that the organism will be rewarded after varying time intervals, so long as it is performing the behavior to be rewarded. This schedule produces a slow, steady rate of response. A *fixed ratio schedule* means that the organism is rewarded after a fixed number of responses or actions. This schedule produces a high, steady rate of responding with only a brief pause after the delivery of the reinforcer. Finally, a *variable ratio schedule* means that the organism is rewarded for varying amounts of work, like pulling the lever of a slot machine. This schedule creates a high steady rate of responding.

Final Remarks

From the behavioral psychology of Watson and Skinner, what one finds is an approach to personality that is very stripped-down and bare bones basic. The formation of a personality is a *very* mechanical, mathematical sort of process. Responses that are made to occur more frequently and intensely tend to persevere, and this makes them more likely to be associated with the particular organism in question. "Personality" is simply a word used to refer to an aggregate of enduring conditioned responses. These responses and the overall pattern that they appear to create are a mere reflection of the environmental conditions that created them in the first place. Personality is not substantive in itself. If you change the environmental conditions, then you will likely change the so-called personality.

The behavioral approach minimizes the possibility of unnecessary obfuscation in one's approach to personality. This is particularly notable with regard to the possibility of positing all sorts of hypothetical mental contents to account for behavior. Behaviorists sought to take the mind out of the running when it came to explanations of personality. Mental processes are rejected, not necessarily outright, but as *a source of explanation* for personality. In fact, it is sometimes said that radical behaviorists see the mind as a black box about which nothing of substance can be said for developing a truly objective science of human behavior. Anything like a mental event must itself be explained on the basis of prior causes that lie *in environmental conditions*. What goes on "outside" the person has overall priority over what goes on "inside" the person.

The radical, strictly behavioral views covered in this chapter can be said to have a zero tolerance policy when it comes to obfuscation via some private world of intrapsychic processes. It is for this reason that individuals like Watson and Skinner dedicated so much of their careers to creating a more streamlined, parsimonious alternative to Freudian psychology, which is the theory that will be discussed next. Of course, one could just as easily argue that Watson and Skinner were guilty of the opposing tendency toward oversimplification. In fact, radical behaviorism has lost much of its power of influence in psychology for just this reason. Behaviorism has largely become *cognitive*-behaviorism, wherein mental processes have been used to augment behavioral explanations of human interaction.

Ironically, the focused effort to take on Sigmund Freud is exactly what makes for deep continuities between the opposing viewpoints of radical behaviorism and orthodox Freudianism. For example, both approaches are rooted in the desire to make psychology a natural science. Both approaches acknowledge that human beings are born with adaptive physiological processes, emphasizing the hedonistic tendencies of human beings. Indeed, in spite of all his distancing efforts, Watson was highly influenced by Freud, especially during the period of his Little Albert studies. That entire line of research was inspired by Freudian thought, as Watson was attempting to provide alternative interpretations to Freudian psychology of how adult personality can be influenced by childhood experiences. Similarly, B. F. Skinner cited Freud more often than any other author.

Suggested Readings

Pavlov, I. P. & Anrep, G. V. (2003). *Conditioned reflexes*. Mineola, NY: Dover Publications.

Skinner, B. F. (1953). *Science and human behavior*. New York: Free Press.

Thorndike, E. L. (1932). *The fundamentals of learning*. NY: Teachers College.

Watson, J. B. & Rayner, R. (1920). Conditioned emotional reactions. *Journal of Experimental Psychology*, *3*, 1-14.

Chapter 4
Freudian Orthodoxy:
The Psychosexual Personality

Like Watson and Skinner, Sigmund Freud wished to create a psychology that was patterned after the natural sciences (e.g., physics, biology, chemistry, and so forth). In what is known as his *project for a scientific psychology*, first conceived in the mid-1890s, Freud called for an approach to psychology that would be firmly based in neurophysiology. Whereas the behaviorists tended to search for the true or ultimate causes of behavior in environmental conditions, Freud was more impressed by the manifold workings of the human organism's internal world. This difference in orientation is reflected in the somewhat divergent paths taken by the behavioral thinkers and Freud. Whereas the behaviorists specifically prohibited recourse to the mind for explanatory principles of behavior, Freud plunged headlong into the "intrapsychic" world of desire, impulse, memory, fantasy, thought, and emotional conflict.

When viewed from the perspective of Freudian psychology, behaviorism appears somewhat shallow or incomplete. The Freudian point of view brings a degree of depth and vitality to the study of personality that is lacking in behavioral psychology. Human beings are understood on the basis of their "inner" lives, which are at once neurological and subjective. Again, this is a difference in emphasis only. Freud was not unaware of the power and influence of environmental interactions. Quite the contrary, his theory involves many complex social interactions. However, whereas behaviorists look upon environmental conditions as the primary cause of behavior, Freudian psychology takes a detour through the biologically influenced *interpretations* of the individual in its search for the causes of behavior. The experience of the person is brought to the fore in psychoanalytic psychology in a way that was inadmissible in behaviorism. For Freud, the passions, desires, and motives of the organism are far too complex and important to be relegated to the so-called black box. An adequate theory of personality must contend with the arduous striving of each individual human being to attain those pleasurable forms of need gratification required for the survival of the individual and the species.

Sigmund Freud's path makes sense considering his beginnings. Freud began his career as a neurologist. In the late 1880s, he became intrigued by certain patients treated by two of his colleagues, Jean-Martin Charcot and Joseph Breuer. These patients displayed symptoms like paralysis, muscle cramps, and seizures, which were believed to be psychological in origin. Impressed by these cases, Freud coauthored a book with Joseph Breuer entitled *Studies in Hysteria.* In essence, Freud and Breuer attempted to explain how the symptoms of this strange psychological presentation (then called hysteria) were the result of having repressed disturbing, traumatic memories. Over the course of his career, Freud attempted to further demonstrate that these memories were actually psycho*sexual* in nature. The terms *sex* and *pleasure* were virtually synonymous in Freud's work. Accordingly, his theory is referred to as a *psychosexual theory*.

When Freud began formulating his psychoanalytic ideas in the late 1800s, his manner of conceptualizing the mind was markedly different from his contemporaries due to the sheer amount of emphasis he placed on the role of unconscious processes in the mental life of human beings. With their emphasis on conditioned responses, the behaviorists shared Freud's belief that behavior is rooted in processes that lie outside of conscious awareness. However, Freud's ideas predate those of the behaviorists, as was noted earlier.

Freud saw the mind as consisting of three layers: *the conscious mind, the preconscious mind,* and *the unconscious mind.* The conscious mind refers to explicit awareness, and consists of those things that have become the object of focal attention. If you can pay focal attention to something, freely and fully examine it with your senses, and articulate your experience in words, it belongs to the conscious mind. As you can imagine, however, not everything in life receives one's undivided attention. There are many things that lie on the outskirts of focal awareness. Anything that has the potential to be given focal attention but is not currently conscious belongs to the preconscious mind. Right now you are not paying attention to what you had for breakfast this morning. But, as soon as you consider what you had, that knowledge moves from the preconscious mind to the conscious mind. Now, once you return to the task of learning about Freud, the knowledge of your breakfast will move back down to the preconscious. For Freud, there is a constant interplay between the conscious and preconscious minds. Such is not the case, however, for the contents of the unconscious mind. The contents of the unconscious are blocked from conscious awareness. The unconscious contains memories and impulses that are unacceptable, dangerous, or otherwise anxiety provoking and are therefore too difficult for the person to acknowledge. They are defensively kept at a distance from consciousness.

Freud explained this *topographical model of the mind* by embedding it with three interactive systems known as the *id, ego* and *superego*. He considered the id to be a repository of animal drives inside a person. Many authors refer to Freudian theory as a theory of "instincts." However, Freud used the German word *Instinkt* somewhat sparingly. He tended to prefer the term *Trieb*, meaning urge, impulse, impetus, desire, or *drive*. Instincts and reflexes were far too rigid to suit Freud's purposes.

The id is the wellspring of libidinal energy or *libido*. Freud compared the functioning of the mind to a hydraulic energy system. The most potent form of energy that pumps through this system is libido. Libido is a Latin word that means wish or desire. For Freud, libido is a person's appetite for pleasure, particularly those forms of pleasure associated with tension reduction. It is aggressive, highly impersonal, and constitutes the majority of the unconscious mind. The id's libidinal energy gives rise to *primary process thinking*. Primary process thinking is a kind of thinking that is rooted in hedonistic and selfish tendencies; it consists of narcissistic fantasy and operates according to *the pleasure principle*. Freud used the term *pleasure principle* to indicate that human beings are creatures who crave immediate gratification from the time they are born. To sum up, the core system of the human mind (the id) houses a force of energy (libido) that unconsciously drives us to get pleasure for ourselves on demand (the pleasure principle).

As is obvious, if everyone were to only act on the basis of primary process thinking there would be no civilized society. Therefore, the id must be restrained. As a result, at some point in the development of the personality, the person has to develop another psychic structure to acquire some means for cooperation with other people. This structure is called the ego. The ego is the source of patience, control, and reason. It is the conflict manager of the personality. The ego refers to the aspect of the mind that realizes that drive satisfaction must be accomplished in ways that are not only effective, but also conducive to having to live with others. This is called *the reality principle* and it governs the functioning of the ego. The ego's functioning enables the person to delay the initial, infantile impulse to get one's own needs met immediately. As a result of ego formation, a new, more mature looking manner of seeking self-gratification emerges which is said to operate according to *secondary process thinking*. The ego thus provides the means for the individual to adapt to the social world beyond early infancy. Aspects of the ego reside on all three layers of the mind. That is, there are aspects of adaptive functioning that are conscious, some that are only preconscious, and some that are unconscious as well.

As the developing person confronts the reality of living with other people, it is inevitable that she will discover that people make value judgments. At some point during child development, the child perceives that words like "good" and bad" are associated with certain behaviors. More importantly, she comes to find that there are punishments associated with the things that are labeled "bad." As a result, it becomes necessary for the child to learn the rules of civilized society so as to avoid punishment. This is the birth of the superego, which is the closest thing to a conscience to be found in Freudian psychology. The person will develop an inclination to appear moral and ethical. This tendency will also need to be kept in check, as too strong a superego would prevent the person from satisfying the id. Like the ego, the superego exists on all three levels of the mind.

According to Freud, the process of adapting to a world that does not permit unbridled immediate gratification is not easy. The development of a personality is fraught with frustration and conflict at every step of the way. The id would like to be satisfied immediately, but the demands of reality and the opposing inclinations of the superego stand in the way. The ego is stuck in the middle of all of this conflict and must find solutions to life's problems. One of the ways that the ego learns to deal with difficult, frustrating life predicaments is to look for people who appear to have developed effective coping strategies and use them as models for one's own behavior. This is called *identification*. However, where the ego cannot find the means to cope with frustration through identification, excessive anxiety may build up and result in the appearance of *defense mechanisms*. Defense mechanisms are strategies employed by the ego to manage anxiety by distorting reality. They tend to operate outside of conscious awareness. That is, they are preconscious or unconscious in nature. These mechanisms cover over both the source of what is threatening to the person and the fact that a cover up is taking place. In other words, defense mechanisms are not just lies, they are lies that the person believes on some level. They are not just deceptions, rather they are self-deceptions as well. Some common defense mechanisms are as follows:

- *Displacement*: Shifting libidinal energy from its original object of choice to something less threatening. (Example: Taking out your hatred for your boss on your children when you come home from work. Your boss can fire you, but your children are easy targets.)
- *Sublimation*: Shifting libidinal energy from its original object of choice to something socially acceptable and productive or creative. (Example: Turning your hatred for your boss into the creative energy that fuels a series of paintings that symbolize the powerful human experience of hatred.)
- *Suppression*: A selective avoidance of alarming, anxiety producing impulses, thoughts, images, or memories. Suppressed information is relegated to the preconscious. (Example: A person sees her cat hit by a car, but refuses to talk about it or even think about the event.)
- *Repression*: The act of repelling alarming, anxiety producing impulses, thoughts, images, or memories away from the conscious mind. Repressed information is relegated to the unconscious. (Example: A person sees her cat hit by a car, but cannot recall the shocking event.)
- *Regression*: The act of retreating from an anxiety-evoking step in development to an earlier period of development. Specifically the person seeks to rely on the coping mechanisms typical of the last period of

development that felt safe. (Example: A young lady who resorts to crying and stomping her feet when her teacher does not allow her to make up an exam.)

- *Projection*: Attributing the source of an anxiety producing impulse to someone else. (Example: A young man with wandering eyes constantly accuses his girlfriend of looking at other men.)

- *Denial (or Disavowal)*: The refusal to acknowledge the reality of a danger or threat. (Example: An alcoholic insists she does not have a drinking problem despite her many alcohol related arrests and health problems.)

- *Rationalization*: Interpreting anxiety provoking impulses or their morally reprehensible consequences as reasonable, logically consistent, and/or ethically sound. (Example: Cutting down your neighbors favorite flowers because you did not like her by noting, "It's the end of the season and this will make them grow back better next season anyhow. I actually did her a favor.")

- *Reaction formation*: The adoption of an attitude or characteristic style of presenting oneself that is the exact opposite of one's true desires, inclinations, or impulses. (Example: Becoming an outspoken radical conservative regarding sexuality when you are actually quite lustful and promiscuous.)

One of the more talked about defense mechanisms pertaining to Freud's thoughts on personality development is *fixation*. Fixation occurs when a developing person refuses to face the challenges brought about by a new stage of life. As a result, she remains at a more primitive state of psychological development. Moving on to a new phase of life can evoke anxiety in a maturing person. Change means that old comforts and previously secured means for libidinal gratification might be threatened. Thus, fixation is usually discussed in terms of its relationship to certain stages of child development that Freud identified. In particular, Freud outlined five stages or phases of psychosexual of development: *oral, anal, phallic, latency,* and *genital*. At each stage of development, the id seeks gratification from a different part of the body called an *erogenous zone*. If the child is under-satisfied or over-stimulated at any stage, she may become fixated on the erogenous zone of the stage in question. Freud's stage theory of development is widely considered critical to his explanation of personality formation. The idea is that the way the child learns to manage physical desires colors or influences the general style of personality that develops. The ways in which we are conflicted, frustrated, and fixated thereby become the defining features of the individual personality. While Freud did mention connections between stages of development and personality types, it was actually a psychologist named Karl Abraham who really articulated this aspect of Freudian theory with some degree of approval from Freud.

The oral stage is the first to appear and is identified with early infancy. The anal stage emerges just before the typical period of potty training for Westerners (between the first and third year). The phallic stage is typically identified as a preschool age period (i.e., three to six). The latency phase is pre-pubescent (six to ten). Finally, the genital stage is associated with puberty and onwards into adulthood. However, Freud believed these stages were only loosely ordered. For Freud, it would be a mistake to suppose that these phases appear in a perfectly clear-cut fashion. One may appear at the same time as another, they may overlap one another, or they may be equally present alongside one another.

During the oral stage, the child seeks pleasure by using the mouth. The mouth can be used to incorporate food to satisfy hunger. However, Freud noted that the child derives such enjoyment from the mouth that she will continue to seek pleasure from that erogenous zone even when there is no longer a need for food. Thus, the child will suck on her hands or use a pacifier. The child can get oral stimulation "receptively" from sucking, licking, and swallowing, or "sadistically" (i.e., aggressively) by biting, chewing, and so forth. Normally parents understand that the child seeks oral pleasure and will try to accommodate the child accordingly. At a certain point, however, parents attempt to wean the child. They try to get the child to stop sucking her thumb, to stop using a bottle, and to stop using a pacifier. If the child is under-satisfied or over-stimulated during this time, an oral fixation may become a trait of the developing personality. The child might go on to pursue pleasure associated with the mouth far beyond the time of the oral stage. This could be done receptively or aggressively. So, for example, the child might grow to be a person who feels driven to smoke or drink or suck on candy, which are *oral-receptive* traits. Freud even considered a gullible person to be oral-receptive, since such a person would "swallow anything," so to speak. On the other hand, the child might grow to be a person with a nail biting habit or become verbally abusive to others, which are *oral-aggressive* traits.

During the anal stage, the child seeks pleasure by holding on to and letting go of waste. There is a pleasure that the child experiences from controlling the stimulation of the anal sphincter muscles. The child is given time to enjoy the pleasure of expelling fecal matter at will through the use of diapers. However, parents know that the child is developing control over the anal region, so they eventually attempt to potty train the child. This can be experienced as a threat to the child's immediate gratification of anal pleasure. Fixations stemming from this stage include anal-retention and anal-expulsion. *Anal-retentive* personalities display stinginess, stubbornness, and an exaggerated tendency toward control, orderliness, and cleanliness. *Anal-expulsive* personalities are just the reverse, displaying excessive tendencies toward impulsivity, disorganization, messiness, dominance, and cruelty.

The phallic stage is the stage where the child discovers the genital zone and the pleasure that can be had by manipulating that area of the body. However, whereas there were outlets for the satisfaction of the oral and anal drives (e.g., pacifiers and diapers), the child is obstructed from manipulating her genitals. Such manipulation is deemed socially unacceptable. This leads the child to conclude (unconsciously, of course) that the key to getting genital satisfaction must lie in relationships with members of the opposite sex. As a result, the little boy seeks to win the affection of his favorite female and the little girl seeks to win the affection of her favorite male (i.e., mommy and daddy respectively). Freud called this unconscious desire to sexually possess the parent of the opposite sex the *Oedipus complex*.

According to Freud, little girls and little boys find female genitalia virtually incomprehensible. Males have penises, and this makes sense to a child. There is a clearly identifiable sex organ. However, female genitalia appear to be missing. There is no clearly identifiable organ. This has far-reaching implications. For the boy, the pursuit of mommy places him in competition with daddy. If the father enforces personal boundaries that let the boy know that he cannot be so attached to mommy his whole life, the boy child will come to experience *castration anxiety*. After all, some people (i.e., girls) are missing their penises! A suspicion that the father might castrate him disposes the boy child to back away from his pursuit of mommy and learn how to attract a woman of his own by identifying with his father. Girls, however, find that they have already been castrated and develop *penis envy*. They enter into competitive relations with their mothers and try to become daddy's girl. In time, daddy has to again enforce personal boundaries so that his daughter will come to identify with her mother and learn how to become a woman to attract a man of her own. In both cases, the parents are supposed to make their children feel special and desirable for a time, but then impose boundaries that allow for a workable resolution of the stage. If this is disrupted, the child may develop an Oedipal fixation, which would become evident in problems revolving around gender, sex, and/or relationships (especially intimate relationships).

For Freud, the first three stages of development were the most important in the formation of the personality. At the fourth stage, there is no erogenous zone that dominates development. The id is restrained and libidinal energy is sublimated into the socially acceptable activities of youth, such as school, hobbies, sports, etc. This all ends, however, when puberty arrives. With the onset of puberty, the genital stage has begun and the child rediscovers the genitals, only now in a more mature, adult manner. However, behavior, mental processes, identity, sexual identity, and so forth are all already well underway by the conclusion of the phallic stage.

Final Remarks

Freudian psychology brings a level of dynamic psychological depth to personality theorizing that is wanting in both genetic and traditional behavioral conditioning approaches. From a Freudian point of view, individuals like Watson and Skinner begin with a valid insight in the fact that human beings are naturally attracted to pleasurable activities, some of which satisfy basic biological needs. However, to then relegate one's understandings of this attraction to the sheer mechanics of positive and negative reinforcement stops short of a full grasp of its profundity. In short, the mental or intrapsychic aspects of pleasure seeking (e.g., the dynamics and folly of the id, ego, and superego) must be taken into account.

For Freud, the biological determines the psychological. In this sense, he is more sympathetic to the genetic paradigm of inheritance. When it comes to human beings, biological development proceeds faster than mental development and thereby colors the final form of the human personality. For instance, the genital region of the body becomes a highly active erogenous zone at the *phallic* stage long before the child comes to grasp the nature of genital functioning or realize the social import of that functioning. It is not until the genital stage that some degree of insight appears, but by that time the form of the individual's personal style has already been set in motion. Moreover, this style has been determined by many interactions that will remain unconscious. Each stage of development marks an attempt to manage a physical need, which then gives shape to the overall experiential and behavioral tendencies of the individual.

Freudian psychology introduces a pronounced element of passion and desire into personality theorizing. His view highlights not only the influential power of hedonistic longing, but also the sheer depth and complexity of mental life. What genetic theorists would see as an inherited trait and behaviorists would describe as the mere result of repeated exposure to environmental conditions, psychosexual theory sees as rooted in numerous intrapsychic interchanges between diverse psychic systems on several levels of awareness.

In spite of these differences, however, it is important to bear in mind that there are also deep continuities between the genetic, behavioral, and Freudian viewpoints covered thus far. All three traditions make an attempt to turn psychology into another kind of natural science. At least in their traditional interpretations, they each prioritize the physical over the psychological. All three traditions see human personality as rooted in and abundantly determined by processes lying outside of conscious awareness and control. Moreover, they see human beings from a primarily self-serving vantage point. In a sense, psychosexual thinking represents a kind of synthetic hybrid of constitutional and behavioral thought. However, one must also bear in mind that Freudian psychology has been reinterpreted in many ways. To be sure, some interpretations capitalize on Freud's tendency to make very existential-humanistic kinds of comments now and again. The fact is, there are many different Freud's depending on what era one is referring to and which insights one cares to highlight out of his works. Similar caution is warranted when approaching trait theory and evolutionary psychology, which are still works in progress.

Suggested Readings

Abraham, K. (1965). *Selected papers of Karl Abraham*. London: Hogarth Press and Institute of Psychoanalysis.

Fisher, S. and Greenberg, R.P. (1985). *The scientific credibility of Freud's theories and therapy*. New York: Columbia University Press.

Freud, S. (1949). *An outline of psycho-analysis*. New York: Norton.

Freud, S. (1960). *Three essays on the theory of sexuality*. New York: Basic Books.

Mitchell, S. A., & Black, M. J. (1995). *Freud and beyond: A history of modern psychoanalytic thought*. New York, NY: Basic Books.

II: COGNITIVE-AGENTIC AND EGO-PSYCHOLOGICAL PERSONALITY THEORIZING

Chapter 5
Rotter, Bandura, and Mischel:
The Cognitive-Agentic Personality

This chapter revolves around insights into personality that have been developed by Julian Rotter, Albert Bandura, and Walter Mischel. At present (2013), these three individuals are still alive. Thus, this chapter will be examining theoretical perspectives that, technically speaking, could still be considered works in progress.

The term *social learning theory* is sometimes used to refer to the kinds of views covered in this chapter. The logic behind the term is that the views presented here emerged from the behavioral tradition in psychology (e.g., Watson, Skinner, etc.), which has sometimes been referred to as *learning theory*. However, it is equally true that social learning theory has moved beyond the strictures of traditional behaviorism by securing a place for the efforts of the socially *interactive* organism amid the determining forces of the environment. The details of what goes on in the mind of the individual are vital to understanding personality, and that sentiment deviates from the traditional behavioral distain for mental processes. At the same time, this does not mean that these theorists are trait theorists. Social learning perspectives seek to avoid the opposing extremes of strict behaviorism which grants overriding priority to the environment and the kind of trait theorizing that grants overriding priority to relatively discrete characteristics of the person irrespective of environmental context.

Since the early days of his work, Bandura's psychology has been increasingly referred to as *social-cognitive theory* to better match the language of the day. By the mid-1980s, Bandura's increasing emphasis on mental or cognitive processes seemed to call for a new, more modern sounding label. Similarly, Rotter and Mischel are sometimes referred to as *cognitive-social theorists* or even *cognitive social learning theorists*. The prioritization of the term *cognitive* would suggest a somewhat tighter focus on the mental or cognitive processes involved in determining the form of personality than what is found in Bandura's works, but one should not make too much of these differences in popular terminology. In fact, some texts will cover these thinkers in the same chapter and refer to all three of them as social learning theorists. The more important issue is that they each see the personality as deeply rooted in environmental contingencies as part and parcel of their behavioral lineage, but depart from traditional behaviorism on the basis of their attention to the cognitive processes used to interpret and frame the context of their behavior. For these three thinkers, behavior and environment alone cannot override all other considerations when attempting to understand human personality. The efforts of the individual organism, her cognitively informed *agency*, are seen as vital to personality formation.

Julian Rotter

Like B. F. Skinner, Julian Rotter believes that a human being evaluates new experiences on the basis of previous reinforcement. Personality is learned. In this way, Rotter is grounded in behavioral theory. However, unlike Skinner, Rotter has held that a person's reaction to a reinforcement depends on its *subjective meaning and importance* rather than on the objective characteristics of the reinforcement only. This insight likely germinated through his contact with George Kelly, the architect of *personal construct theory*. For Rotter, the motivation to continue or abandon a course of behavior depends, in part, on goals. Human motivation, human behavior, and human personality are goal directed, which is an insight he took from the individual psychology of Alfred Adler. According to Rotter, reinforcement is most effective when the reward in question promises to bring the person closer to her personal goals.

In the context of Rotter's theory, prediction is indicative of understanding. This is far from certain, of course. It is possible to discover certain methods of prediction without having achieved a deep grasp of an issue. Nonetheless, the notion that prediction indicates understanding has a certain pragmatic appeal because it bears with it the possibility of control. Pragmatism is a deeply rooted value in both American culture at large and those forms of psychology that are patterned after the natural sciences. Being an American, natural scientific psychologist, Rotter naturally places high value on prediction. Thus, his theory has a tendency to sound formulaic. At the same time, Rotter has legitimately attempted to provide a cogent account of the dynamics of personality formation as these dynamics play out in the context of environmental conditions.

Julian Rotter has offered two schemas or frameworks for the prediction of behavior. One framework allows us to size up the probability of an individual engaging in *a particular behavior in a specific situation*. The other framework is designed to help us get a reliable sense of the behavioral tendencies of an individual *in general* (which comes closest to the business of understanding the relatively consistent patterns of behavior called *personality*).

Rotter uses the term *behavior potential* (BP) to refer to the probability that a particular response will occur at a specific time and place. According to Rotter, behavior potential is a direct function of both *expectancy* (E) and *reinforcement value* (RV), giving rise to the heuristic formula, $BP = f(E + RV)$. Expectancy refers to a person's expectation that reinforcement(s) will occur in a given situation as a result of the behavior in question. This insight is essentially Skinnerian. However, unlike B. F. Skinner, Rotter does not believe that one's expectation of reinforcement is based solely on one's history of reinforcement. Skinner's worldview is too passive for Rotter, who sees more interactive involvement in the reinforcement process among human beings. Rotter allows for the possibility that an individual's cognitive appraisal or interpretation (whether rational or irrational) of the potential for reinforcement will ultimately determine her expectancy. This opens the door to the possibility that a person could have been reinforced for a past behavior, but commit a form of cognitive bias (e.g., focus on the negative) that dissuades her from performing that behavior once again. Or, in contrast, a person could have never been reinforced for a behavior but remain convinced that she will eventually be rewarded for it.

Reinforcement value is the preference a person attaches to a specific reinforcement. It is what gives the reinforcement its particularly rewarding character. As was stated earlier, if the particular reward in question is highly valued by the individual, ostensibly because it is congruous with her life's goals, then the reinforcement will be notably rewarding. When the probabilities for the occurrence of a number of different reinforcements are all equal, it is the reinforcement value that best allows us to predict the direction of behavior. Thus, in contrast to Skinnerian theory, the very nature of any given reinforcement is a matter of interpretation and active personal perception. Skinner only discussed the more or less objective aspects of reinforcement, which is referred to as *external reinforcement*. However, when a reinforcement is preferred due to the fact that it is interpreted as meeting the individual's personal goal structure, this is referred to as *internal reinforcement*. Taking his analysis a step further, Rotter notes that there are factors that tend to determine a person's goal structure as it relates to the potential to engage in a particular action at a particular time. For example, Rotter observes that one must understand the individual's personal *needs* at the time and place in question (e.g., Is she hungry? Is she generally insecure?). Moreover, one must ask about the total, *psychological situation* that this person is in, since goal structures are not determined by personal traits alone, but also by the person's interaction with specific environments, which could lean her in the direction of wanting certain things over others (e.g., Is she fighting with her boyfriend via text message? Has she happened upon a mob scene?).

To understand the behavioral tendencies of an individual in general (rather than specific tendencies in a very particular situation), Rotter says that one must appreciate the general needs that all people seek to fulfill. For example, human beings need to gain *recognition* or achieve some level of *social status*. Humans need *to feel dominant* and believe that they have a certain degree of *control* over others. Human beings seek to achieve a sense of *independence, protection, love, affection,* and *physical comfort.* Each need can be satisfied with a whole host of behaviors. General needs such as these are the keys to understanding people's goals, since they tell us about the kinds of motives that can potentiate action. In order to refer to the potential that a group of functionally related behaviors will be undertaken to satisfy some need, Rotter used the term *need potential* (NP). As for what determines whether or not a person will be acting on one or another need depends on two factors, each of which is analogous to an element of Rotter's formula for predicting specific behaviors.

For Rotter, need potential is a function of *freedom of movement* (FM) and *need value* (NV), giving rise to the heuristic formula, $NP = f(FM + NV)$. Freedom of movement refers to one's overall expectation of being reinforced for one's actions, meaning that it is analogous to what was previously referred to as expectancy.

Need value refers to the degree to which the person prefers one set of reinforcements (associated with certain needs) over others. Need value is thus analogous to what was previously referred to as reinforcement value. Together, need potential, freedom of movement, and need value comprise the individual personality's *need complex*.

Before moving on, it ought to be noted that Rotter's personality theory relies on the notion of *locus of control* in assessing both specific and general behavioral tendencies. Locus of control is perhaps the most famous concept of his entire approach to personality. According to Rotter, people come to develop a sense of where the control over their circumstances lies. They develop a sense of whether or not the control over punishments and reinforcements lies within them (i.e., an *internal locus of control*) or outside of them (i.e., an *external locus of control*). Locus of control is thus the degree to which people perceive a causal relationship between their own efforts and environmental consequences. Accordingly, a person's locus of control has a direct impact on expectancy and freedom of movement, depending on the level of analysis in question.

Albert Bandura

Albert Bandura's departure from traditional or "strict" behaviorism can be illustrated by considering the behavior of smoking cigarettes. Typically, when an individual takes a drag from a cigarette and inhales the smoke into her lungs for the first time, she experiences things like burning, nausea, light-headedness, and a foul taste. If we were to use the language of operant conditioning theory, one would say that the act of taking a drag off of a cigarette is immediately followed by a set of consequences best understood on the basis of positive punishment. According to traditional behaviorism, punishments suppress behavior. Yet, it is quite common for a person to take yet another drag, then another, finish the cigarette, and then try it again.

This is puzzling. At this point, one would have to do some clever maneuvering in order to explain this behavior using the traditional behavioral concepts of reinforcement and punishment. For example, one might wonder if there are really a number of powerful unconscious or non-conscious reinforcements affecting the person's nervous system that go undetected. In this case, it would only *appear* that the drag off the cigarette had a primarily aversive effect on the surface. Such an explanation would lead us to a viewpoint that moves closer to Freudianism or neurological psychology. Or, perhaps one could explain the behavior on the basis of the possibility that there are people in the individual's environment reinforcing her with praise or some other form of rewarding attention. This is quite possible.

While Bandura was aware of these possibilities, he developed another line of thinking. Bandura proposed the idea that there are reinforcements, overlooked by traditional behaviorism, that nonetheless exert a powerful influence on people and provide a fuller explanation of something like smoking again after being punished. According to Bandura, it is important to note that an individual's patterns of action are not only influenced by the reinforcements and punishments that she has received directly. A person is also influenced by the rewards and punishments that she has witnessed *other* people receive for their actions. Thus, Bandura's work is sometimes referred to as a *theory of observational learning*.

Modifications in behavior that occur as a result of having witnessed *someone else* get reinforced are called *vicarious reinforcements*. Social learning thus begins with the observation of a model of behavior or *role model*, as it is more commonly known. This model of behavior can be internalized by the observer, mentally represented, and remembered. At this point, the observer may develop a cognitive expectancy of being rewarded for performing that same behavior. If the behavior appears viable under the right circumstances, the observer would thus imitate the role model in order to be directly reinforced, which is a process known as *the modeling effect*.

According to Bandura, human beings tend to model their actions after those who appear skilled, competent, or otherwise powerful in some way. In other words, we use those who appear to be the most capable of obtaining reinforcement in a given setting as our template for future courses of behavior. Conversely, people who lack competence or who are otherwise lacking social status in a given setting are the most likely to look to others for a model of behavior. Moreover, modeling is more likely to occur in situations where individuals have no frame of reference for differentiating between appropriate and inappropriate behavior. Such situations are inherently disempowering and evoke a general sense of uneasiness, which results in the search for a competent model of behavior. This explains why it is that children are so "impressionable," as is often said. Due to their age, children are inherently less experienced than adults and often have no frame of reference for how to behave in various circumstances. They are thereby disposed to see adults as more competent and look to them as role models.

As is obvious, Bandura's theory relies on numerous factors that are cognitive in nature (e.g., observation, perception, mental representation, memory, and cognitive expectancy). His thinking became even more cognitive in orientation when he observed that modeling is more likely to occur when the observer perceives the witnessed behavior and its consequences to be *valuable* in a given circumstance. The question of values strongly implicates the beliefs and views of the individual. As a consequence, Banudra transformed a highly anonymous, depersonalized tradition of behaviorism into an approach to personality that begins to scratch the surface of what is "personal" in personality. Older forms of behaviorism were sometimes referred to as S-R theory, meaning a stimulus gives rise to a response. Bandura's theory, on the other hand, has been referred to as an S-O-R theory, where the "O" refers to the involvement of the individual organism.

These days, the word *person* is often used in lieu of the word *organism* when referring to Bandura's viewpoint. Bandura explains personality functioning in terms of *triadic reciprocal causation*, which implicates three factors in the final determination of personality. He saw personality as originating within the context of an interactive system of *environment, person*, and *behavior*. Here, S-O-R (stimulus-organism-response) becomes E-P-B (environment-person-behavior). By integrating the concept of "person" into his thinking Bandura wished to emphasize that humans have some capacity to select or restructure their environment so that certain things are picked out, paid attention to, valued, and remembered for future reference.

Bandura identified a number of "personal" factors that govern the process of observational learning. As was alluded to earlier, in order for the modeling effect to occur, a person would have to pay *attention* to a potential role model. The person would also have to mentally *represent* the model of behavior and *remember* this model's actions in some way. In addition, the observer would have to develop some kind of expectancy or *anticipation* of being rewarded for the behavior that has been witnessed. Moreover, this reward must appear *valuable* to the observer in order to mobilize her *motivation* to emulate the role model.

Should the reward be deemed valuable, the observer will approach or withdraw from the possibility of action on the basis of four additional factors. To begin with, her *social status* will be implicated. All things being equal, a person with less social status would be more likely to emulate a model of behavior emanating from a person with more social status. However, this assumes that the individual with less status feels that she would be able to perform the behavior without negative consequences. She would thus need to have the requisite *self-efficacy* to attempt the proposed behavior. Self-efficacy is a term that Bandura introduced into his theory to refer to the belief in one's ability to succeed in carrying out specific tasks. It is essentially skill-specific self-confidence (rather than a global judgment). A person can have high-efficacy in one situation, but low-efficacy in another. In addition, there is the issue of *behavioral production*. This means that the person has to find workable answers to the question, "How can I accomplish this?" Finally, the person has to engage in the requisite *planning* in order to carry out the behavior in question.

All of these factors are indicative of the *agency* inherent to the personality in question. Bandura's theory is agentic in the sense that things like attention, mental representation, value judgments, planning and so forth involve effort on the part of the person. In particular, Bandura noted that the agency of the person is grounded in four major factors. First, people do things deliberately. This is called *intentionality*. Second, people set goals for themselves based on desired outcomes and select behaviors that they believe will produce these outcomes. This is called *forethought*. Third, people monitor their progress as they attempt to fulfill these goals. This is called *self-reactiveness*. Finally, people think about and evaluate their motives, their values, and the meaning of their goals. This is called *self-reflectiveness*.

Having endorsed this apparent degree of self-control and self-determination, Bandura held that, in addition to observational learning, human beings are capable of *enactive learning*. This is learning that occurs as a result of having thought about and evaluated the consequences of one's own behavior. At this point, it might be tempting to assume that Albert Bandura is an advocate of the notion of personal freedom or freewill in decision making. However, it is interesting to note that Bandura has explicitly rejected the notion of freewill. This is strange considering his apparent advocacy of an active, agentic organism in his model of triadic reciprocal causation. Bandura considers people to be proactive, self-regulating, and self-reflective, and this would otherwise be an implicit advocacy of some measure of personal freedom. The fact is that his explicit denial of the notion of freedom comes as a result of his desire to maintain his reputation as a descendent of natural science. Thus, Bandura has referred to freedom of the will as an antiquated relic of medieval philosophy. He considers the notion of freewill to be superficial, Pollyanna, and undisciplined since people obviously act from within a nexus of environmental exchanges and influences. However, those personality theorists who advocate for some degree of freewill agree with Bandura on this last point, and in the end, Bandura has made what philosophers call a *straw man argument* against freewill. That is, he has painted a mere caricature of freewill that is easy to discredit in order to maintain a certain kind of reputation as a scientist.

Despite this problematic meta-theoretical issue, Bandura has provided some highly practical insights concerning the ways that personal efficacy can be acquired or enhanced. According to Bandura, the most influential source of self-efficacy is successful performance, which he called *mastery experience*. In other words, when hard work leads to success, the result is increased self-efficacy. Various states of arousal and emotionality can affect performance and thereby have an impact on self-efficacy as well. So, in order to build self-efficacy through mastery experiences, it is helpful to know the kinds of physical and emotional states that are optimal for the task in question. One's performance will also have to be judged as successful if one is to experience increases in self-efficacy. Thus, one's *personal standards* ought to be realistically gauged to the difficulty of the proposed task. Further, one ought to be able to regulate one's *self-reaction* or emotional response to one's own performance.

Self-efficacy can also be enhanced through social means. For example, *social modeling* and *social persuasion* can increase self-efficacy. In the case of social modeling, Bandura observed that a person's belief in her abilities can be strengthened by observing other people similar in overall competence and social status perform a task successfully. Social persuasion refers to the idea that self-efficacy can be increased through verbal support from other people. Bandura also believed that self-efficacy can be modified via *proxy agency*, wherein an individual enlists the help of others. This aspect of his theory is illuminated by the old adage that there is strength in numbers. Personal efficacy can be enhanced through group membership, assuming that the group in question possesses a superior degree of collective efficacy. However, this is not a guarantee. Bandura has noted that various social forces have been posing obstacles to the development of both social and personal efficacy. These include the changing nature of an increasingly diverse society, our reliance on rapidly changing technologies, complex and slow social machinery (i.e., "red tape"), and mounting social problems.

Walter Mischel

Like Rotter and Bandura, Walter Mischel believes that human beings *interact* with the environment in a *meaningfully coherent* way, such that there is "internal" structure to the personality. Traditional behaviorism envisioned personality as a set of reactions that occur at the mercy of environmental contingencies. Mischel, however, feels that behaviorism created a conceptual framework that allowed behavior to shift too freely in the hands of the surrounding situation. As a result, older versions of learning theory would be inadequate for understanding the stabilizing structure inherent to personality.

At the same time, Mischel stands opposed to those attempts to account for this stabilizing structure in the manner of a so-called "trait" theory. Trait theory moves in the opposite direction of traditional behaviorism. Trait theorists attempt to identify the basic ingredients (i.e., "traits") that constitute personality irrespective of situational variables. Gordon Allport spearheaded this tradition, but he eventually amended his original approach to traits to become more context sensitive and individualized. However, the same cannot be said for those who have come after Allport, most of whom were unaffected by Allport's change of heart. To review, Allport began by compiling a master list of thousands of words used to describe an individual's personality characteristics or traits. However, later trait theorists used a mathematical procedure called a factor analysis to whittle down these thousands of traits to much smaller trait categories of varying sizes. Their attempts have been to isolate those traits that tend to be more responsible for the variations in behavior found in samples of research participants (e.g., liveliness, vigilance, dominance, privateness, openness to experience, neuroticism, extraversion, agreeableness, conscientiousness, psychoticism, and various others). Like Allport, however, Mischel considers personality structure to be too context-dependent to be understood on a recipe-styled trait basis. Traits cannot by themselves account for personality.

For Mischel, the relative stability of the personality can only be found in *psychologically meaningful personality signatures,* which are always only expressed relative to environmental contexts. These signatures thus have an *if-then* character about them in the sense that *if* the environment presents in one way, *then* one behavior might occur, but *if* the environment is different (or is perceived as different), *then* a different behavior will be elicited. This conceptualization therefore allows one to grasp situation-based differences in behavior but still allow for the possibility of an underlying structure that provides unity to the personality.

As an interactionist, Mischel does not want to simply abandon the idea of stable personality characteristics. Rather, he believes that researchers should pay attention to both situational and personal characteristics that influence behavior (i.e., attention, goals, values, expectancies, feelings, etc.). Personal traits are meaningful and motivating, but only given the right set of circumstances. Personality signatures are too context-dependent to be isolated and quantified the way a trait theorist would have it. Personality is dynamic. It is the result of a complex, interactive system of *cognitive-affective units* resulting in an interactive *cognitive-affective personality system.* This systems view allows that a person's behavior might change (sometimes drastically) from situation to situation, but in an always-meaningful way that is comprehendible if one were to study the individual's stable *life-patterns* of reacting to the world.

What are life-patterns made of or built from? Mischel has identified five *cognitive-affective units* (i.e., emotionally toned psychological building blocks) that he believed to be the core structures responsible for personality formation and personality functioning. The first cognitive-affective unit is called *encoding strategies* and refers to how a person selectively pays attention and conceptualizes the world. It includes her personal constructs about self, others, and reality at large. So, a person's self-concept and general ways of categorizing or classifying things in the world (situations, events, interactions, and so forth) would all be included here. The second cognitive-affective unit is called *competencies and self-regulatory strategies* and it refers to a person's beliefs concerning her skills, plans, and strategies for carrying out life goals. It includes an individual's expectations of success as well, so it would be related to concepts like locus of control and self-efficacy. The third cognitive-affective unit is called *expectancies and beliefs* and it includes a person's expectations regarding the consequences of specific behaviors, whether or not they will result in reinforcement or punishment. The fourth cognitive-affective unit consists of a person's *goals and values*. The final cognitive-affective unit is a person's *affective responses*. This refers to the way a person feels about the consequences of her actions, her self-reaction, and the overall emotional tone that permeates the cognitive systems noted here.

Final Remarks

Rotter, Bandura, and Mischel see people as subject to the forces of conditioning, but not in an exclusively automatic way. What they add to personality theorizing is an appreciation of the degree to which human beings actively interact with the environment. The social cognitive learning perspective sees human beings as goal-directed, cogitating animals whose active interpretations of events are at least as important if not more important than the objective features of the events themselves.

With Rotter, Bandura, and Mischel, the personality has become self-informed and agentic or self-regulating. Through their works, behaviorism has become more intrinsically harmonious with

Alfred Adler's individual psychology, the developmental works of Jean Piaget, and the ideas of clinicians like Aaron Beck and Albert Ellis among others. Perhaps no other theory comes closest to the perspectives discussed in this chapter than George Kelly's personal construct theory. For Kelly, the processes inherent to personality functioning are "psychologically channelized" or set on a relatively consistent course via the typical ways that the person *conceptualizes* and *anticipates* events. A human being develops a *construction system* that varies as she successively reconstrues and reconceptualizes events that yield varying results. The person chooses for herself those constructs that appear to have the greatest potentials for the development, extension, and progressive redefinition of the construction system and, by default, the personality. With regard to issues of individual choice, however, Kelly is likely closer to Alfred Adler than Rotter, Bandura, or Mischel.

All in all, Rotter, Bandura, and Mischel can be said to have taken behaviorism to new levels of sophistication. They have provided a wealth of information concerning the "inner," subjective, or personal structure that undergirds the overt behaviors that have been the focus of traditional behaviorism. They have allowed us to develop a deeper understanding of the pragmatic goals and aims inherent to personality where there had previously been but an accumulation of unconscious reactions. The personality is now seen as capable of emotionally colored information processing and agentic self-regulation. In fact, it would not be inaccurate to say that Rotter, Bandura, and Mischel collectively bring personality theorizing to the threshold of *genuine* self-determination, dare they admit of it. At present, this has yet to be seen.

Suggested Readings

Allport, G. W. (1955). *Becoming: Basic considerations for a psychology of personality*. Connecticut: Yale.

Allport, G. W. (1968). *The person in psychology: Selected essays*. Boston: Beacon Press.

Bandura, A. (1977). *Social learning theory*. Englewood Cliffs, NJ: Prentice-Hall.

Kelly, G. A. (1963). *A theory of personality: The psychology of personal constructs*. NY: Norton.

Mischel, W. (1971). *Introduction to personality*. NY: Holt, Rinehart and Winston.

Rotter, J. B. (1982). *The development and applications of social learning theory: Selected papers*. NY: Praeger.

Chapter 6
Erik Erikson: The Ego and the Psychosocial Personality

Whereas Rotter, Bandura, and Mischel bring a more multifaceted style of analysis to traditional behavioral theory, Erik Erikson can be said to have done the same to Freudian psychoanalysis. He is not the only thinker to have done so, but his adaptation of Freudian psychology is an exemplary analogue to the way that the cognitive social learning tradition adapted traditional behaviorism. Rotter, Bandura, and Mischel moved behavioral thought away from its narrow focus on external reinforcement toward a heightened appreciation for the ways in which human beings make plans, pursue goals, uphold values, form beliefs, derive perceptions, and so forth. Through their efforts, human personality is better understood in its active, adaptational aspects rather than only its passive, hedonistic aspects. The same can be said of Erikson's reinterpretation of Freudian theory.

Erik Erikson grounded his approach in the psychosexual theory of development put forth by Sigmund Freud. For Freud, all experience and behavior were interpreted from the point of view of animal drives or the id. In the end, personality was essentially a function of its biological substrate. Far from recognizing the *centrality* of the social aspects of human development, Freud's interpretation of human beings focused on individuals' drives to attain pleasure. Erikson sought to go beyond Freud by integrating a more profound respect for the role of the ego and its attempts to come to grips with the demands of its social milieu into psychoanalytic theory. Thus, Erikson's approach is called both an ego psychology and a psychosocial theory.

Like the cognitive social learning theorists, Erikson was explicit that his work was a particular attempt to account for the relationship between the agency of the individual person and her social surroundings. Coming from the psychoanalytic tradition, however, Erikson spoke of this relationship in terms of ego processes. Erikson identified ego processes as those functions that serve to bring organizational unity to the biological and social systems inherent to the personality. So, for example, biologically speaking, a human being develops a need for sexual gratification. However, this need announces itself among a community of other people with a similar need for which a whole host of social norms, mores, beliefs, laws, aesthetics, and so forth have been created. The personality is ever-socialized, and personality development is predetermined to grow in the direction of a widening circle of social relations. Throughout life, then, the individual's sex drive will have to be managed and made commensurate with the social world in which she lives. This is the job of the ego. As Freud had asserted, the ego is the managerial aspect of the personality.

Erik Erikson revisited Freud's stage theory and placed more emphasis at each stage on the needs of the ego and its repertoire of interpersonal relations throughout the development of personality. As a result, he modified the approximated time ranges for the stages somewhat. At each stage of development, Erikson saw the child as needing to resolve a particular ego "crisis" in social and emotional development. He used the term crisis to refer to a radical turning point in development. According to Erikson, all of the issues of all of the stages are present in some form at the outset of development, but they nonetheless get their own special time period to take center stage in accordance with *the epigenetic principle*. As Erikson articulated it, anything that grows does so according to a predetermined plan. Out of this plan, each part arises and has its own special time of ascendancy until all the parts have become unified within a multifaceted, functioning whole. In Erikson's theory, a successful resolution of any ego crisis means that the child will begin to develop new ego qualities and psychological strengths that will allow her to advance to a new, more multifaceted stage of development. Should a failure to resolve an ego crisis occur at any stage, the child will become fixated at that stage or regress to issues of the previous stage, as was the case in Freud's theory as well.

For Freud, the child's id seeks libidinal satisfaction via the mouth during infancy (i.e., licking, sucking, biting, chewing, and swallowing). As is the case at each psychosexual stage, the child requires gratification, but not to excess. Moreover, the child cannot be traumatized, abused, neglected, or in any other way denied adequate satisfaction. If the child is overindulged or undersatisfied, then the child is liable to develop a fixation. At this stage, fixations come in the oral-aggressive and oral-receptive varieties. Whereas Freud emphasized the child's oral pleasure seeking during this stage, Erikson chose to highlight the extreme dependency that the child experiences during this time. Due to this extreme sense of vulnerability, the child's ego seeks out *consistent, predictable nurturance* from caregivers. Starting with Freud's emphasis on the role of feeding, Erikson noted that while the id needs oral pleasure, the child's ego is in need of a sense of the mother's caring dedication to feeding (and her needs in general). Should the child find her caregivers to be responsive and committed, she will develop an adequate sense of trust in herself, others, and the world. In addition, she will develop the strength of *hope*, which acts as the foundation for all future development and socialization. Thus, Erikson saw the first stage of development as a time where the child must resolve the ego crisis of *basic trust versus basic mistrust*, which comprises the first year of life. However, should some form of emotional neglect prevent the child from developing a basic sense of safety in the world, she will come to rely heavily on attempts to withdraw from shared reality in order to attain a sense of security. For Erikson, an example of the kind of pathology that results from a fixation at this stage is infantile schizophrenia.

In the event that the child successfully resolves the first ego crisis, she will move on to stage two. Erikson called the ego crisis of this stage *autonomy versus shame and doubt*, which spans from the first to the third year. During this stage, Freud emphasized the child's attempts to obtain an adequate sense of pleasure via the anal sphincter muscles despite parental attempts to enforce potty training. Fixations due to inadequate parenting at this stage included anal-retentive and anal-expulsive character types. What Erikson chose to focus his attention on during this stage of development was the fact that potty training revolves around the issue of control (an ego quality). With bodily maturation, the anus becomes one of the first major things in the child's life that she can have control over. However, as soon as parents see this potentiality becoming actualized, they seek to use their authority to teach the child the socially acceptable way to regulate bowel movements. If the child comes to feel that the parents are not trying to dominate her, but are ultimately attempting to help her develop *self-control*, the child will develop a sense of autonomy. In addition, the child will develop the strength of *will*, which is the foundation of notions like freewill and goodwill that always seem to be the subject of meta-theoretical debate. However, if parents are emotionally insensitive in their child-rearing tactics, the child will not develop a sense of personal authority. Rather, feelings of shame and doubt will erode the child's sense of agency. For Erikson, the kinds of pathology that would result from a fixation at this stage include impulse control disorders and obsessive-compulsive neurosis. Alternatively, if the emotional neglect that the child endures during this stage proves to be overwhelming enough, the child may regress back to problems of the previous stage. Such is the case with every new stage.

Erikson saw the ego crisis of the phallic stage as one of *initiative versus guilt*, spanning from the third to the fifth year. During this developmental period, the genital region of the body comes into focus. Freud showed us that the Oedipal dream manifests itself. The child needs to feel like the beloved mommy's boy or daddy's girl for a time and then have this dream manageably come to an end by identifying with the parent of the same sex. If this fails to occur, the child may develop a host of difficulties revolving around relationships, gender, and sexuality. Failures from the previous stages will become more pronounced in the personality. At the same time, however, the child is developing a new sense of mobility. The child is developing new mental and physical skills that give her the ability to envision and undertake projects of her own planning and creativity. According to Erikson, if the child is allowed to enjoy these new abilities under the caring *direction and guidance* of her parents, then she will develop a sense of initiative. Moreover, the child will develop the strength of *imaginative purpose*. However, should parents rely on excessive punishment and guilt rather than involvement in their child rearing, initiative will not develop. Rather than being motivated to become involved in projects and relationships, the child will be burdened by a looming sense of guilt over acts contemplated and undertaken. For Erikson, an example of the kind of pathology that results from a fixation at this stage is hysterical neurosis.

During the latency period, the ego crisis that arises for the child is *industry versus inferiority* ranging from the fifth to about the eleventh year of life. For Freud the latency period was a time when the instinctual urges of the id were sublimated. The child is learning how to be like mom or dad, practicing the skills needed to become a young man or woman. Erikson believed that during this time the ego is attempting to attain a sense of *mastery* in using the body as a tool for building an identity via work and play activities. According to Erikson, the child requires encouragement and sometimes sensitive instruction or "coaching" to accomplish this task. If the child finds that she can successfully identify with her physical and mental abilities and feel at home in her body, then she will develop a sense of industriousness. In addition, she will develop the strength of skillfulness or *competence*. However, if the child encounters some difficulty during this period, industry will not develop. Rather than becoming enterprising and diligently involved with tasks, the child will develop a pervasive sense of inferiority.

Erikson characterized the stage five ego crisis as one of *identity versus role confusion*, which begins with puberty (about eleven or twelve on average) and ends around eighteen years. Freud saw this stage as the time when the genital region is rediscovered, only now in a more adult fashion. Adult sexuality comes into focus and genital maturation brings about a radical change in priorities and lifestyle. Dating and group affiliation become more important and soon, others (the adults) will be looking to the young person to make decisions concerning things like college, career, and so forth. In order to tackle these challenges, Erikson saw the child as needing a strong *commitment* toward the establishment of a sense of identity. Lifestyle choices like who to date, who to befriend, whether to have a family, and what job to pursue all require that the young person figure out who she is. However, Erikson noted that the task of achieving a constant sense of identity is dependent upon both dedication *and* the success of past stages. In puberty and adolescence all the resolutions of previous stages are more or less questioned again. Adolescents have to refight many of the battles of earlier years. So, for example, the basic trust of others that was won in infancy has to undergo new testing as the adolescent is forced to put her emotions on the line and trust a potential significant other when dating for the first time. Thus, failures throughout development would increase the probability of social difficulties and prolonged role confusion in adolescence. If, however, there is a successful resolution of the ego crisis of identity versus role confusion, the strength of *fidelity* will arise. The young person will experience the kind of resoluteness and perseverance necessary to figure out who she is supposed to become in her adult years.

As a young adult, the person moves into the stage of *intimacy versus isolation*, which spans from approximately eighteen to thirty-five. It is common that the search for that special someone to settle down with begins in young adulthood. However, as Erikson saw it, a sense of identity is a prerequisite for a stable, functional relationship with another person. Emotional intimacy with another human being involves *sharing* who one is as well as knowing what one desires from a relationship. However, these things are out of reach for a person who has yet to establish an identity and commit to a lifestyle. The person who can find the courage to use the newfound strength of fidelity to make genuine commitments to others will eventually discover who she is meant to be with and experience real intimacy. This would mean a successful resolution of the ego crisis of intimacy versus isolation and the strength of *love* would arise. However, the person who cannot commit to others will eventually come to experience a sense of loneliness and isolation.

In middle adulthood, from about thirty-five to fifty-five, the person begins the stage of *generativity versus stagnation*. The period of middle adulthood is often the time when a person makes their mark on humanity and becomes most *productive* in her career and personal life. If fidelity is used during this time period as a commitment and devotion to one's creative, constructive potential, there will be a successful resolution of the ego crisis of generativity versus stagnation. As a result, the strength of *care* will emerge. If, on the other hand, the person is lacking a stable identity, is lazy, is disappointed in her choices, or is settling for lesser goals in life, she will experience a global feeling of stagnation.

Toward the close of the lifespan, the person enters the stage of *integrity versus despair*, which is from fifty-five onward. According to Erikson, the person is now confronted with the task of developing a sense of *meaningful perspective* on the life that she has lived. She needs to be able to proudly accept the life she has lived with the people she has lived it with. Perhaps with the help of sensitive others, she can experience a feeling of comradeship with all of humanity and a deep faith in the meaning of her life. This is what is meant by integrity. It amounts to a meaningful old age and a dignified exodus from this world. If there is successful management of the ego crisis of integrity versus despair, the strength of *wisdom* will be apparent. Since death now waits in the wings, the only other alternative would be disgust over a wasted life and despair over its untimely end.

Final Remarks

Erik Erikson's psychosocial ego theory contributes significant experiential breadth toward an understanding of the adaptational efforts inherent to personality formation. Erikson's contribution compliments the somewhat more intellectual, computational sounding focus of cognitive social learning theory in illuminating the pragmatic functioning of human personality. Erikson's approach alerts us to the fact that successful personal and social adjustment requires qualities like basic trust, autonomy, initiative, industriousness, identity, intimacy, generativity, and integrity to emerge from within a field of growth-conducive social relations beginning with the mother-child dyad. Erikson noted that personality development is in fact rooted in a kind of maternal conviction, a mother's belief that her parenting is a deeply meaningful activity. This conviction will be communicated to her child by permeating her actions throughout development. This then acts as a template for adaptive social relatedness in ever-widening circles over the course of the lifespan. In contrast, psychological dysfunction is rooted in disruptive, maladaptive social conditions that give rise to basic mistrust, shame and self-doubt, guilt, inferiority, role confusion, isolation, stagnation, and despair.

To reiterate, Erikson's overriding focus was the *adaptive* efforts of the personality as exemplified by the integration of biological and social functioning. This is the typical sort of focus of cognitive and ego psychological theories. Like most such theories, Erikson's approach does not contain a focused, unabashed attempt to *dwell* on the very *core* of human personality, to focus on what is most *personal* in the personality. As the existential developmental psychologist Richard T. Knolwes once noted, Erikson never pursued the full significance of the strengths that he mentioned in connection to a successful resolution of each ego crisis. Yet, it is here, with the identification of these strengths or virtues that Eriksonian theory actually leaves the typical foci of cognitive and ego psychological theorizing and begins to integrate aspects of the truly human into personality theory. It is with hope, will, imaginative purpose, competence, fidelity, love, care, and wisdom that Erikson opens the possibility of appreciating the full complexity of personality. For example, Erikson's notion of an interpersonally mediated freewill that comes to the fore during the second stage of development not only remediates the meta-theoretically contradictory notion of agency found in cognitive social learning theory, but also presents personality theorizing with the challenge of understanding the intricacies of socially embedded self-determination. All in all, Erikson's basic strengths move personality theorizing in a more self-psychological and interpersonal direction, yielding an increasingly multifaceted, dynamic, and holistic understanding of human personality.

Suggested Readings

DeRobertis, E. M. (2008). *Humanizing child developmental theory: A holistic approach.* New York: iUniverse.

Erikson, E. H. (1961). The roots of virtue. In J. Huxley (Ed.), *The humanist frame* (147-165). NY: Harper and Brothers.

Erikson, E. H. (1963). *Childhood and society.* New York: W. W. Norton.

Erikson, E. H. (1968). *Identity: Youth and crisis.* New York, NY: W. W. Norton.

Knowles, R. T. (1986). *Human development and human possibility: Erikson in the light of Heidegger.* Lanham, MD: University Press of America.

III: INTERPERSONAL PERSONALITY THEORIZING

Chapter 7
William Stern and Gordon Allport: The Personal Personality

This chapter begins a full-fledged journey into the realm of the personal in personality. The kind of personality theorizing represented here comes from what is called the personalistic tradition in psychology. Contrary to the way it sounds, the tradition of personalism is not individualistic in nature, but places rather heavy emphasis on self-world-other *relationships*. The term *personalistic psychology* is most closely affiliated with the work of William Stern and one of his students, Gordon Allport, who will be the subjects of this chapter. William James and Alfred Adler are the other two seminal figures responsible for the emergence of this tradition of thought.

In the previous section, it was noted that individuals like Rotter, Bandura, and Mischel highlighted the agentic goal orientation inherent to personality formation, while Erik Erikson added significant experiential breadth to this viewpoint. For all of these thinkers, the goals inherent to personality formation can be said to be oriented toward the attainment of various kinds of reinforcements and adaptive life skills, but Erikson pointed toward a new horizon. Erik Erikson characterized a psychosocial integration inherent to personality that ultimately gave rise to character strengths suggestive of the spontaneous, creative, and owned nature of personality formation. This serves as a point of departure for the thinkers in the current section, beginning with Stern and Allport.

Similar to the way that Erikson employed his psychosocial model, Stern and Allport provide an integrative foundation for their respective approaches to personality. Both Stern and Allport viewed personality as psychophysically neutral, meaning that personality is not a certain psychic something locked inside of a person's cranium. Psychophysical neutrality is a concept used to indicate that personality is best understood on the basis of manifold worldly relations. Person and world are said to *converge* via the medium of characteristically *unique* projects and relationships that, under healthy conditions, are as spontaneous, creative, owned, and deeply valued as Erikson suggested.

William Stern

Despite having been a brilliant philosopher and psychologist, William Stern remains an underappreciated figure in the history of both philosophy and psychology. This is especially the case in American psychology where Stern's name and legacy appear to be narrowly associated with the concept of IQ. This not only diminishes Stern's contributions to psychology on the whole, but also gives the erroneous impression that his approach to psychology was exclusively psychometric in nature. Quite the contrary, William Stern has had a compelling influence on the third force (i.e., humanistic or "human science") approach to psychology through the highly respected work of Gordon Allport.

William Stern's approach to personality stems from his general philosophical and psychological viewpoint known as *critical personalism*. Critical personalism refers to the philosophically rigorous and scientifically disciplined study of the person envisioned as a *unitas multiplex* or multifaceted whole. Stern proposed critical personalism as an alternative to the philosophical and scientific tradition of *atomism*, which habitually overlooks the dynamic world-relatedness of the person as such in its impulse to dissect human beings into discrete parts and anonymous part-functions. At the same time, critical personalism offers an alternative to homunculus spiritualism, where the "person" is reduced to the status of a ghost residing inside or alongside of a mass of physiological systems. This viewpoint is sometimes referred to as intellectualism, rationalism, or dualism.

According to Stern, a *person* is a *psychophysically neutral* being. A person is not a body and a mind "stuck together," but a functional whole. A person is a being that is composed of many different parts, but nonetheless forms *a unique and intrinsically valuable unity*. Even though a person displays numerous part-functions in the form of things like physiological processes, intellectual processes, and so forth, she is able to achieve a unifying, "goal-striving self-activation." In other words, a person is a being that is capable of taking up and pursuing goals of her own accord.

Her many different psychological and physiological capabilities are mobilized and brought together in the service of attaining particular goals, thereby giving rise to a *novel life form*. Personhood is *a goal-related achievement*, one that opens the door to the possibility of developing a *personality*. Stern defined personality as *a living whole that, through its own efforts, strives to realize enduring aims, goals, and purposes.*

William Stern introduced the concept of *convergence* into psychology as part and parcel of his holism. For Stern, heredity and environment taken alone or combined in a simple additive fashion were equally untenable. The notion of convergence was employed to emphasize the fact that the distinction between these two forces had been made based upon their prior, dynamic interrelatedness in the life of the functioning person. Attributes that have been customarily referred to as belonging to *nature* and *nurture* simply cannot exist as unadulterated elements of an otherwise random or purely mechanical structure. "Nature" and "nurture" actually emerge in and through the concrete activities of the growing individual. Stern's position was thus that the psychologist must first determine the goals and aims of the total organism as the requisite context within which to interpret the relative manifestations of so-called nature and nurture, which are merely abstractions unto themselves. The developing person is the fundamental unity or *Gestalt* that founds analyses pertaining to inheritance and learning.

All in all, Stern considered the person to be a genuine unity comprised of many facets and forces that play across the individual's environmentally situated body. Moreover, the ever-present striving toward organized functioning in the world is itself a real causal force in the development of the personality. According to Stern, the integrative becoming that characterizes personality development is a stratified system consisting of *phenomena* (i.e., experiences), *acts*, *dispositions*, and the "I" (i.e., the subject or *self*). Stern considered the relationship between these constituents to be a "layering" of sorts, a hierarchical organization. Each dimension of the person's development is inherently related to each other, but is not reducible to any other. Perceptions and other experiential phenomena occur against the backdrop of actions. Actions do not occur randomly (at least not under normal or healthy circumstances), but in accord with dispositions and goals, irrespective of whether these dispositions and goals are clearly articulated or unreflective.

Particular goals are themselves organized and contextualized via an overarching goal system (the self-system) that maintains the order and overall integrity of the personality in its worldly interactions. Stern rejected any strict bifurcation or dichotomy of self and world. There is no homunculus or "little man" nestled inside of the person orchestrating behavior. He believed that the study of personality ought to be approached interpretively as it actually operates in the world. In his view, we must see the personality as oriented to the specific context within which it is embedded, never otherwise. The person's behavior always occurs against the background of a unique "field of projection." The convergence of person and world completes the essence of the individual personality.

Since persons are always caught up in their worlds, Stern held that human awareness is "graded," meaning that one's knowledge of things can range from very diffuse (or *embedded*) to very vivid and sharp (or *salient*). Accordingly, a person may interpret events, objects, others, and so forth in a manner of embedding within or withdrawing (i.e., making salient or abstracting) from one's own situatedness in the world. Stern's notions of embeddedness and salience are indicative of a perspective that views the awareness of self and world as many-layered. Stern was explicit that there are "subconscious" aspects to the mind, broadly construed. There are latent dimensions of experience and "supra-conscious" aspects of being in the world that are as yet out of reach. Stern thus displayed a certain sympathy toward psychoanalytic thinking about the mind without resorting to the contradictory sounding notion of an *un*conscious mind. This style of thinking is repeatedly illustrated in Stern's attempts to explicate the teleological (goal directed) nature of personality formation. He saw personality as inherently goal oriented, but insisted that goal *consciousness* does not have to accurately represent the person's goals. In fact, dispositions, goals, and their teleological ends may have nothing to do with direct consciousness whatsoever. Persons can pursue goals without being reflectively aware of what they are up to.

Stern's belief in the inherently goal oriented nature of personality is also indicative of the active, spontaneous, creative nature of personality. For Stern, the notion of a purely passive personality runs contrary to human nature. The person is simultaneously an agent and the receiver of the passive givens of experience. The person's experience of the world cannot be adequately understood in purely passive terms because of the *synthetic activity* inherent to each person's worldly relatedness (referring to a capacity for acts of organizational synthesis or integration). In Stern's view, any and all phenomena of experience require both an individual subject and an act in which each experience is embedded. The inherent interconnectivity of acts and phenomena (experiences) is itself embedded in a network of dispositions and goals. The activities that provide the occasion for experiences occur in accord with plans, aims, and purposes, whether articulated and unarticulated. Moreover, dispositions and goals themselves cannot be merely explained away via biology or even psychology. According to Stern, the developing person as a whole comes more and more to operate in the service of *supra-individual tasks*, goals that are not reducible to perfectly law-like biological or psychological processes. Against reductionism, Stern insisted on the possibility of freely willed acts.

The relative freedom of the will in Stern's work is not merely a freedom *from* conditions, but more importantly a freedom *for possibilities for growth and maturity*. Drawing on the Aristotelian notion of *entelechie*, Stern considered personality formation to be part and parcel of the psychophysically neutral manner that humans as a species continually project themselves toward goals, aims, and ends in the world. Actions ultimately serve the actualization of potentials for relatively ordered, organized becoming (as opposed to conflict, disorder, or stagnation). As the psycho-neural organization of the personality complexifies it functions more and more in the interest of selective perception and self-regulated action (though not in any individualistic sense). Personality integration is thus dynamic and motivational. Wholeness is an ideal that the person actively pursues in Stern's view. Individualizing form and goal-striving activity are inherently and inextricably interrelated. It is in and through the integrational impetus that the person realizes her potentials for growth and maturity.

According to Stern, both the goals and general value orientation of each person are particular to her personality. That is, the living individual is the primary principle of organized becoming throughout the process of personality formation. Hence, Stern warned psychologists against too hastily leaving the domain of direct experience in order to posit abstract, artificial "law-like" principles to explain personality functioning. An individual's personality cannot be understood solely as an instance of abstract laws such as those one might attribute to the rest of the natural world. The person is always a unique and intrinsically valuable unity and needs to be studied as such.

To be sure, Stern believed that the unique and intrinsically valuable unity of the person could only be accurately portrayed when her *manifold* strivings are taken into account. He spoke of the multiplicity of psychological dispositions as a kind of overabundance to be ordered by the "I" or self in the direction of growth and maturity. He observed that many enduring characteristics are required to scaffold personality formation.

Stern classified the various goal oriented strivings that characterize personality formation, the major two being strivings toward *autotelie* and *heterotelie*. Autotelic strivings consist of goals that promote individual development (i.e., self-maintenance and self-development). Heterotelic goals, however, extend beyond the self and consist of progressive tendencies belonging to different subclasses depending on their nature. In particular, Stern identified *hypertelie*, *syntelie*, and *ideotelie*. Hypertelic goals are those that join the individual with the unity building goals of family, folk, humanity, or Deity. Syntelic goals are those that join the individual with the unity building goals of her peers. Finally, ideotelic goals pertain to the realization of abstract ideals (e.g., truth, justice, etc.). In and through heterotelie, the individual is prevented from being a closed system of self-concern. As personality formation proceeds, behavior becomes increasingly multifaceted or diversified. Personality development is a dynamic, flexible process of moving from more simple to more complicated forms of organized world-relatedness.

Gordon Allport

Gordon Allport defined personality as the dynamic (i.e., complex, plastic, and changing) organization within the individual of those psychophysical systems that determine her characteristic (i.e., unique) behavior and thought. The term psychophysical is used deliberately to call attention to the idea of psychophysical neutrality that was introduced by William Stern. For Allport, like Stern before him, personality is a relative unity comprised of many hierarchical organized, intertwined facets. In Allports work, these facets include things like reflexes, drives, intensions, habits and attitudes, traits, and selfhood.

Reflexes are the more or less automatic actions of the body, including conditioned responses as defined by the behaviorists. Drives are highly flexible, species-wide innate behavioral tendencies, each of which has adaptive value for the organism, as Freud had shown. Allport readily acknowledged the many pertinent insights into personality submitted by both the behavioral and psychoanalytic traditions. Intensions include the hopes, desires, wishes, ambitions, aspirations, and plans of the person. Habits were given a place in Allport's thinking via the influence of John Dewey, whom he admired very much. Habits are not the ingrained result of mere repetition, though they can begin that way. Rather, habits are *selective* regularities in behavior. Habit implicates learning, which includes more than the simple repetitive associations that behaviorists characterized. Habits are specific to very particular kinds of life situations, like the habit of taking one's vitamins or of performing an exercise regimen. Attitudes also create regularities in behavior, similar to habits, but attitudes are predispositions to judge or evaluate specific things, people, events, situations, and so-forth.

Traits are similar to both habits and attitudes by the fact that they are unique or defining behavioral predispositions, but they are more general in nature. When multiple habits are joined together, traits are the result. Similarly, when an attitude is increasingly generalized to more and more things, it takes on the characteristic generality of a trait. Allport was enamored with traits because he felt that in their generality, they were highly revelatory of the relative consistency inherent to personality on the whole.

Allport divided traits into two main categories, *common traits* and *personal dispositions*. Contemporary currents of so-called trait theory focus on common traits. In their defense, Allport believed that common traits could be studied through *nomothetic* research methods (i.e., methods aimed at discovering law-like regularities) where the very same trait is comparatively displayed by numerous individuals or entire groups of people. However, this research strategy will not be without its problems, as traits are not discrete entities with sharp boundaries separating them from one another. Trait categories are abstracted consistencies gleaned from the real lives of human beings acting amid worldly predicaments and situations. He would have agreed with Walter Mischel that the identification of behavioral regularities is a context-dependent affair.

For Allport, the most important structural aspects or building blocks of the personality are personal dispositions, which require the use of idiographic (i.e., case sensitive research methods) to capture the subtleties of their individuality. He believed that every person has hundreds of unique dispositions, but also held that about five to ten of them are the most central to each personality. Thus, he distinguished between *cardinal, central,* and *secondary dispositions.* A cardinal disposition refers to an eminent characteristic or ruling passion so outstanding that it dominates one's life. These are rare. A central disposition refers to the five to ten most outstanding aspects of a person's lifestyle. Secondary dispositions refer to those less conspicuous, but nonetheless present traits that people display under varying conditions, of which there can be hundreds.

On the whole, some traits are motivational and lead to the initiation of action, whereas others tend to be more stylistic and guide a course of action. Whether motivational or stylistic, however, some traits are experienced as incidental to one's being, while others are felt to be close to the core of who one is as an individual (i.e., the one's we most closely identify with). This latter group of traits are thus said to be affiliated with the self or *proprium* of the personality. Allport called the proprium *the individual quality of organismic complexity displayed by a person.* It refers to that which has experiential warmth and sense of importance to one's personal integration and global personality formation. Propriate traits are highly individual as a matter of course. However, there are several major aspects to propriate functioning across individuals, which tend to be largely responsible for the unity, wholeness, integration, order, and organization of the personality.

Allport identified eight dimensions of the proprium. The first is a unified *bodily sense*. Another word for this dimension is coenesthesis, which refers to overall or general sensibility (rather than a localized sensation in a part of the body). The second dimension is *self-identity* or continuity in time and space. The third dimension is *ego-enhancement*, which is a term often used to refer to unabashed self-seeking or egoism. The fourth dimension is *ego-extension*, which refers to becoming identified with things and others in the world. The fifth dimension is *rational agency*, meaning a reason-informed potential to manage needs emanating from both within and outside the person. The sixth aspect of the proprium is *self-image*, which Allport considered to be the most imaginative aspect of the proprium. Self-image refers to one's aspirations of who to become relative to who one is currently. The seventh dimension is *propriate striving*, which is the motivational component of the proprium. For Allport, human motivation involves tension creation as well as tension reduction. Thus, personality cannot be fully understood on the basis of drive mechanisms and homeostasis. Human beings strive to create healthy tensions or optimal states of arousal. The final aspect of the proprium is *the knower*, which refers to the reflective, intellectual appropriation and ownership of one's propriate functioning.

Due to the warm, personal, owned nature the proprium, Allport noted that certain kinds of activity are automatically disqualified from propriate functioning. These include reflex behaviors, basic physiological needs and drives, blind conformity to tribal customs and conditioned habits, inherited psychological characteristics, and compulsive symptoms of illness. The disqualification of this last form of activity is revelatory of the health-oriented focus of the proprium and of Allport's theorizing in general. According to Allport, it is a natural tendency for humans to develop an ever-increasing, differentiated stockpile of traits that will then require coherent unification to allow for ordered functioning and self-expression in the world. This is a dialectic of dividing and uniting that ultimately amounts to an inherent *growth* orientation at the heart of personality formation. Long before Abraham Maslow or the "positive psychologists" ever discussed human well-being, Allport sought to outline the general characteristics of a healthy personality.

Gordon Allport identified a number of aspects inherent to the healthy personality. Giving all due respect to the psychoanalysts, Allport noted that a healthy personality would tend to be rooted in a *trauma-free childhood*. This provides for the possibility of developing *emotional security* and *self-acceptance*. This sense of security gives the person the confidence to *participate in events outside themselves*. For example, the person would display the *capacity to love others* in an intimate and compassionate manner. The person would also have *insight into her own behavior* and have a *non-hostile sense of humor*. Allport also observed that a healthy personality is characterized by a *realistic perception of the environment*, but one that does not preclude a highly imaginative *unifying philosophy of life*.

Allport further asserted that a healthy personality is *motivated by conscious processes* in day-to-day living, though he did not deny the existence of an unconscious mind. In Allport's view, personality theorizing should not be bifurcated along the lines of an overall emphasis on conscious versus unconscious motivation. Rather, the healthier the personality, the more likely it will be that the individual is capable of conscious acts of self-determination. Healthy individuals engage in *proactive behavior* rather than merely reacting or "responding to stimuli." The more disturbed the personality, the higher the likelihood that actions will be unconscious and feel automatic or "compulsive" in the generic sense.

Finally, Allport insisted that a healthy personality is not exclusively motivated by past events, but also by present interests and future aims. A personality is not a sum total of past experiences playing out in the present. The past acts as a foundation for personality, but the person continues to actively build beyond this foundation. So, for instance, a hunger drive can motivate a person to learn how to grow fruits and vegetables. However, this behavior could eventually give rise to an interest in the pastime of gardening above and beyond the original motivation to eat. Allport referred to this tendency for activities to transcend their original motives *functional autonomy*.

Final Remarks

From Stern and Allport comes an approach to personality that places clear and strong emphasis on the notion that individual personalities are unique and intrinsically valuable unities embedded within specific world-relating contexts. Personality is in each case a *unitas multiplex* comprised of numerous world-relating potentials such as reflexes, drives, experiences, intensions, acts, habits and attitudes, common traits, personal dispositions, and propriate (i.e., self) functioning (consisting of a unified bodily sense, self-identity, ego-enhancement, ego-extension, rational agency, self-image, propriate striving, and a knower).

Of all these world-relating potentials, propriate/self functioning deserves special mention. The notion of selfhood highlights the integrative, interactive dynamics that stand at the heart of personality formation. "Self" is a word used to designate the core interactive system of the personality whereby hierarchical organization and dynamic stability are derived. William Stern and Gordon Allport both provided clear indications that this system is imaginative, synthetic, meaningful, and goal oriented by its very nature (i.e., *autotelie, hypertelie, syntelie,* and *ideotelie*). This sentiment is intimated by Alfred Adler, who sought to explore the emergence and functioning of the goal-striving creative self in personality formation. For Adler, the creative, synthetic potential of the self is a direct function of a social context.

Suggested Readings

Allport, G. W. (1955). *Becoming: Basic considerations for a psychology of personality*. Connecticut: Yale.

Allport, G. W. (1968). *The person in psychology: Selected essays*. Boston: Beacon Press.

Stern, C. & Stern, W. (1999). *Recollection, testimony, and lying in early childhood (law and public policy: Psychology and the social sciences)* (James T. Lamiell, Trans.). Washington, D.C.: APA.

Stern, W. (1924). *Psychology of early childhood*. New York: Henry Holt and Company.

Stern, W. (2010). Psychology and personalism (James T. Lamiell, Trans.). *New Ideas in Psychology, 28,* 110-134.

Chapter 8
Alfred Adler:
The Interpersonally
Creative Personality

As the father of *Individual Psychology*, Alfred Adler is commonly known as a psychoanalytic thinker. What is somewhat lesser known is that Adler was a highly original thinker who had an enormous influence on third force psychology. Individuals like Abraham Maslow and Rollo May considered Adler part of the humanistic movement (broadly construed) from the beginning of its development.

Adler's personality theory is grounded in a theory of child development. At the outset of the lifespan, human beings are quite helpless and dependent for a long time compared to other living organisms. This basic fact struck Alfred Adler as highly important and highly neglected in psychology. Personality development receives its *initial* impetus by the drive to overcome *feelings of inferiority*.

According to Adler, there are certain factors that will increase the likelihood that a child will be able to overcome feelings of inferiority. The first of these is a genetic factor: the inheritance of a healthy body. This provides a feeling of physical strength. The second factor concerns the child's environment: primary caretakers who can help her to manage life's challenges with increasing independence. This provides a feeling of emotional stability. The final factor involved in overcoming feelings of inferiority is the developing person's evolving *creative power*. Through creative power, the child will eventually begin to envision and pursue a future wherein she is no longer weak or inferior. Adler called this vision the person's *final fiction*, due to its origins in the creative imagination. However, in order for this vision to provide genuine relief from feelings of inferiority, Adler insisted that the final fiction must be guided by community feeling or *social interest*, as he called it. For Adler, inferiority can only be truly overcome if a person looks outside the scope of their own self interest for fulfillment throughout development.

Adler's entire approach to personality formation is emphatically holistic and field theoretical (i.e., context-oriented). The unity of the person is prioritized over any "part," part-process, or summation of functioning parts. Alfred Adler expressed the fundamental unity of the person prior to any psychological analysis of parts with the term *style of life* or *lifestyle*. For Adler, lifestyle denotes the existential unity of the person and is superior to any psychological concept that would define the personality as a totality in the abstract. That is, lifestyle is *existential* because it is a term used to describe the child's concrete involvement in the world.

In Adler's view, development is a matter of forming larger, more complex wholes, constructing relations between mind and body, over time, in the world with others. Adler's did not shy away from the question of "who" develops, the question of the subject in integrative human becoming. Adler was unsatisfied with strictly genetic, psychosexual, and behavioristic explanations of behavior, and in his quest to avoid atomistic reductionism he asked *who uses* the "raw materials" of human development. As a result, Adler found selfhood to be an inescapable phenomenal reality of personality development.

In stark contrast to the misguided tradition of searching for the self in discrete psychic processes or physical localities, Adler used the concepts of *self* and *lifestyle* almost interchangeably. The formation of a lifestyle is virtually synonymous with the consolidating efforts associated with selfhood. Adler maintained that the raw material of psychology should be *relationship* and *not* the isolated individual. The self is always a relational reality. Adler never used the concept of self as a convenient, elusive homunculus for explanatory purposes. The self is not "structurally absolute" in Adler's works. Adler saw the person as simultaneously shaping and being shaped by others. The person is an inherently social being, thoroughly socialized and subject to the imaginative dynamics of many minds. To state the matter more strongly, it is dubious to point to characteristics of a person and label them the mere results of heredity, for example, because all of a child's traits emerge in and through her concrete interactions with others. For Adler, what is innate via inheritance is never immediately visible but always intermingled with the mutual relation of self and other. Every tendency that might have been inherited has been adapted, trained, educated, and made over again in a field of worldly interactions. To be sure, Adler believed heredity to be an important, influential force in the development of a child. However, he also felt that inheritance tends to be overemphasized due to a neglect of the fact that heredity is always *radically contextualized and made meaningful through environment, circumstance, concrete experiences, and personal history*. Every aspect of a person's lifestyle is in contact with the world.

The intimate intertwining of selfhood and lifestyle in Adler's works gives his thinking on personality formation an unmistakably dynamic, worldly character. The self is meant to refer to the person moving in her uniquely creative manner toward relative integration within a sociocultural context. Integration is not presupposed as a primordial fact of physical reality but an emergent, relational reality. Selfhood always denotes an interpersonally embedded, world-relating psychological organization that is goal oriented. Although the person's organizing, integrating efforts begin early in life, Adler did not consider them to be fixed. Adler believed very strongly that goal setting is fluid and changeable throughout the lifespan. This fluidity is directly related to the creative power of the individual.

According to Adler, the integrating efforts of the person are creative efforts. Nowhere does the uniqueness of a person's lifestyle appear more clearly than in the products of her *imagination*. According to Adler, the person uses her creative power in the formation of goals, which thereby structure her lifestyle. Integrated human living emerges through the establishment and pursuit of existential projects or imaginative projections in time. The creative power of the self in Adler's work is not a mysterious, unscientific concept, but a self-evident characteristic of beings who live in a world that is partially of their own design. Humans *co-constitute* their worlds. For Adler, creative power is the existential, experiential wellspring to be tapped for the initiation, direction, and modification of goal setting. Creative power is evident in the particular manner in which the person manages the struggles of her set of worldly circumstances. This management implicates not only behavior but experience as well. Stated differently, how the person comes to strive and struggle toward personal unification throughout the lifespan involves interpretation and is therefore a matter of *perception*, as well.

For Adler, the individual's total style of life ultimately arises from the way she organizes and perceives the world and from what therefore appears to her as "success." The person lives in a realm of *meanings*. The person does not experience "pure" circumstances; she always experiences circumstances in their personal significance via an interpretive act. Interpretations are used specifically for the discovery of new meanings. Interpretation enlists the creative power of the child, and her individuality manifests in both what is perceived and how it is perceived. Adler asserted that perception is much more than a simple physical phenomenon; it is a psychic function from which one may draw the most far-going conclusions concerning psychological life.

Adler defended the very humanistic notion that a person does not relate to the world in a purely predetermined manner but rather according to a creative appropriation of life's raw materials. Heredity and environment provide the building blocks of development, but are insufficient in and of themselves to account for the course of personality formation. Although such sentiments would normally appear uninformed in an age of ever-expanding brain imaging technologies and high-powered genetic research, recent trends in psychology like dynamic systems thinking have been heading in this very direction for years now. For example, child psychologist Esther Thelen has made a convincing case that change throughout the lifespan is not the result of a genetic program or mere conditioning, but rather the result of "improvisation." Years before anyone ever heard of dynamic systems thinking in psychology, Adler admonished that a person is not a calculating machine but an actively striving organism that tries out different alternatives to find satisfactory means for self-enhancement already in infancy. It was in this regard that Adler developed a deep respect for the importance of play in childhood. Adler believed that a child greatly benefits from having been given the time and space to play because in this space the child is empowered to freely develop creative power and practice goal setting. Through play the child imagines, creates, and practices self-expression with comfortable distance from the preestablished meanings of the adult world.

Creativity and goal setting are perhaps the two most vital

concepts in Adler's thinking on personal integration. For Adler, to say that a person is goal oriented means that she pursues immediate goals simply due to being an active, creative, purposeful organism as well as a final goal that is dimly perceived in its origin, but worked out over time during the lifespan through intermediate goals. On the basis of its goal directedness, Adler saw personality formation as teleological in nature, though he proposed no homunculus to account for this goal directedness. Goals emerge from field of embodied movement in time and space that is decidedly non-mechanistic, fundamentally different from the activity of a computer in that Adler never assumed that the pursuit of goals was always thematic, thought out, or even conscious. The consciousness of a person's goal is always relative and dynamic rather than the clearly conceived aim of an unsituated mental executive. Adler believed that considerations of a real life person involved in her circumstances should be free of scientific bias. In advance of description, there should be no positing of static, unchangeable laws believed to govern behavior, thereby "stacking the cards in advance" of the person's actual striving. For Adler, the ever-present goal is ever in flux. This is not to say that general principles cannot be derived by observing the behavior of a person. Rather, Adler's position was a polemic against biased observation that overlooks *human* behavior in all its intricacies. Unbiased observation, he believed, would account for the creative power of the individual to "cast into movement" all the potentials and other influences inherent to her unifying, goal setting efforts as they unfold over time.

Adler saw the pursuit of goals as arising from a lived sense of incompleteness (i.e., "inferiority") that has its origins in embodied movement. Adler believed that movement stood at the heart of mental development. The ability and urge to move oneself gives rise to the finer details of consciousness. The power to move is the very impetus for motives. Self-movement founds the inclination toward goals, plans, and ultimately the creative discovery of meaning. Thus, physiology and psychology require one another. Furthermore, embodied action has a certain existential priority over intellection in Adler's works. Movement gives rise to attention, the creative impetus, intension, goals, and decisions, each of which unifies living, breathing person. For Adler, "laws" of movement and the language of the body provide more information about a person's direction in life than her words alone. A person's *organ dialect* consists in varied forms of meaningful bodily expression.

If it has not become obvious by now, Alfred Adler believed that humans are capable of free decision. He was opposed to the notion a human being has nothing original to contribute to the course of her development. As was mentioned earlier, he opposed "stacking the cards in advance of development" and saw the evolution of personal freedom as beginning in childhood. This is one of the more controversial aspects of his work. A reason for this is that Adler tended to speak in extremes when making assertions that carry significant societal import. This writing style is perhaps best understood as a consequence of the priorities of Adler's own lifestyle. Adler's life was one of dedication to the welfare of mankind. He was deeply concerned with the welfare of children and how those children become the leaders of tomorrow. He was strongly invested in helping parents and teachers work efficiently and effectively with "pampered" children and "problem" children. He was not as concerned with impressing academicians as much as he was interested in overcoming the deleterious effects of their folly. Consequently, he sometimes felt the need to express ideas in the manner of an impassioned "battle call" rather than a calm, cool, logical inference. Maintaining a clearly identifiable, consistent style of argumentation throughout his writings was, therefore, not always as much of a priority as was his desire to speak strongly and directly to those entrusted with the mental health of children. As a result, one can notice in Adler's arguments against genetic reductionism, for example, just as much weight given to the potential for adults to skirt the responsibilities of child care on the basis of genetic explanations for behavior as the sheer logical untenability of a genetically reductive argument.

Returning to the issue of freedom, one can find Adler asserting that children use their genetic endowment and environmental affordances "freely," while elsewhere he will characterize *the environment* as the decisive factor in determining the child's lifestyle. He will make note that the behavior of a child is "never causally determined," yet elsewhere he admits of "self-created causality." This is sometimes confusing to readers who do not have a holistic grasp of his writing and its associated aims. Simply put, freedom and causality are neither all-or-nothing issues in

Adler's works, nor can his work be adequately characterized from within a dualistic "determinism vs. indeterminism" conceptual framework. Adler advocated a position of limited-freedom with regard to personality. He felt this way about adults and children alike. Adler did not believe that human experience and behavior are utterly and completely determined until some point labeled "adulthood" wherein freedom appears from out of nowhere. Rather, Adler's view on the matter of freedom in childhood tended to mirror what is perhaps a commonsense view of the topic. Using the "freedom implies responsibility" model, we give children far more latitude to make mistakes than adults because we know that they do not possess the same *degree* of freedom as we adults, but we still assume that they are capable of some degree of self-determination.

Against "hard," biologically reductive determinism, Adler insisted that the brain is the *instrument*, not the origin of the mind. He foresaw the coming of "enactive" approaches to neuroscience inasmuch as he held that personal perception is not merely an anonymous, mechanistic "process in the brain," but a kind of activity carried out by the person as a whole. For Adler, students of heredity misguidedly "work backwards," as it were, deducing the cause of behaviors associated with a more or less "finished" product back to a single kind of precursor. This is fallacious reasoning through sloppy induction and hasty generalization. Adler was further aware that some forms of psychology advocate a hard determinism consisting of a purely materialist combination of both "nature" and "nurture." He found this position equally untenable because of the fact that this kind of interactionism is too often defended on the basis of statistical probability alone. To infer strict, materialist causality from statistical probability alone ultimately amounts to a *non sequitur*, meaning it does not logically follow of necessity. Thus, Adler denied materialistic determinism to make room for the active, spontaneous, original contributions of the child as a potent force in the nexus of influences that constitute personality. Adler admitted of causality, just not reductive, materialist forms of causality. Adler acknowledged that both heredity and environment partly determine the creative power of the self, which is a little-known fact about Adler's worldview. When he spoke of self-created causality, he did so with the assumption that it emerges dynamically from within a network of meaningful influences.

Adler stressed the fact that a person is born with a certain body and into a certain familial and cultural milieu that was not of her own choosing. In fact, Adler did not speak of freedom in relation to the very outset of development. Rather, he spoke of the child's body, the child's social position (including birth order), and the characteristics of those responsible for educating her as equal determinants of development. Freewill emerges from out of a context consisting of "alluring and stimulating" forces from both inside and outside the child's body. Of all these contextual forces, Adler was most impressed by the role of the child's social environment and her relationships with others. Adler constantly pointed to the critical role of the child's concrete circumstances throughout development, which he considered to be thoroughly interpersonal. In Adler's view, it is the responsibility of adults to first orient the child's innate creative power in the direction of social interest. At the beginning of personality development the child looks to the adult for help and direction. It is the parent's job to help the child envision a final fiction on the basis of a lifestyle firmly rooted in social interest. According to Adler, any child born with a properly functioning brain and body has a natural inclination toward the development of cooperative relations with other people. However, this inclination is not an instinct or even a drive in the Freudian sense. There is no guarantee that a child will develop a tendency toward cooperation and community feeling (i.e., social interest). To reiterate, however, situations in and of themselves are not what Adler considered decisive for understanding personality, but the person's evolving *interpretation* of her circumstances. Adler analyzed developmental phenomena from a *teleo-analytic perspective.*

Another reason why Adler's thoughts on freedom of the will are sometimes confusing to readers is that he considered freewill to depend on the relative health of the person. Thus, although he tended to argue in favor of the notion of freewill, one can find passages in his works where he opposes the notion of freewill. Adler held that there are many factors that can impede healthy personality development, such as pampering, exaggerated physical deficiencies, and various forms of emotional neglect resulting from defects in economic, social, racial, or family circumstances. Such factors can intensify feelings of inferiority and transform into an *inferiority complex* characterized by a compulsive need for *personal superiority*. In other words, they have the power to influence the person in the direction of deriving "mistaken meanings" concerning her relations with others, meanings that promote egotism and personal superiority while truncating social interest and cooperation. When a person becomes trapped by the allure of egotism, she habitually interprets social situations in a manner that is fraught with anxiety, giving rise to knee-jerk reactions designed to make her *superior to others*. Because of the "automatic" nature of these desperate reactions, the person's behavior is far less spontaneous and conscious than the behavior of a person with social interest. The personality will be characterized by a rigid, perfectionistic lifestyle that alienates others, increases isolation, and continually worsens inferiority. To be sure, Adler considered compulsive behavior to be a warning sign, an indicator of the beginnings of neurotic development. However, if a person's social context is welcoming, supportive, and nurturing, then freewill is more likely to emerge. All things being equal, the older, better educated, and more properly supported the individual, the more likely one is to find compelling evidence of relatively free, relatively conscious self-determination.

Because Alfred Adler was so emphatic about the importance of social relations in the formation of the personality, he gave some attention to the role of *birth order* in child development. Unfortunately, this aspect of Adler's theory has been widely misunderstood and falsely exaggerated. According to Adler, birth order does have an influence on personality development, but it can only be properly understood on an individual basis. The reason for this is that the child's actual "position" in the family is not dictated by the chronological order of birth alone. In addition to the mere fact of birth order, the child's position in the family is the result of several factors, including one's style of attachment to primary caretakers, one's relationship to siblings, and the number of years between siblings. Adler insisted that there are no "fixed rules" concerning this complex aspect of social development. Nonetheless, he did point out some general trends concerning birth order under average circumstances.

According to Adler, an oldest child becomes accustomed to being the center of attention, but is then suddenly ousted from that privileged position. An oldest child will thus have to manage the feeling of no longer being special. If the parents do not prepare the oldest child for this feeling and then neglect the child upon the arrival of the new child, certain detrimental outcomes may arise. For instance, the child may hold a grudge against the mother due to being "pushed into the background," so to speak. The child may then look to the father for companionship and emotional healing. The child may fight against being pushed into the background by acting out in disobedience. The child might even become a habitual "problem child." Through adolescence and into adulthood, such a child would be at higher than average risk of suffering from emotional problems or engaging in criminal behavior. On the other hand, if parents prepare the oldest child for the arrival of a new baby and continue to make the child feel secure, the occasion of the new arrival may simply pass without incident. In fact, Adler believed that if parents properly prepare the oldest child for the arrival of a sibling and ensure a feeling of being loved after this arrival, the oldest child might develop a notable talent for organization and a marked striving to protect others.

In Adler's view, only children are in much the same position as the oldest child. In addition, however, they are the most likely to display obvious signs of the Oedipal struggles noted by Freud. With no other siblings to intrude on their ambitions, only children are at risk for entering into competitive relations with parents.

Stereotypical second child behavior tends to occur when a child is born into a family with siblings who are relatively close in age. Adler believed the best spacing between children was approximately three years. When the spacing between children reaches four to five years and beyond the child will actually experience a blend of both a first and second child's predicament. For Adler, a second child is born into a less stressful situation than a first child assuming that there is no rivalry forced upon the second child by a neglected first born. Being a second child brings with it certain advantages. Being a second child means having to learn cooperation early on in life. In addition, the second child already has a role model in the first born. The first born child sets standards of excellence for the second child and provides a model for the means for meeting life's challenges. Adler was most optimistic about the situation of a second child on this basis. He considered the second child to have the greatest potential for success under average circumstances. He also considered the second child to be the least likely to become a problem child.

All things being equal, the youngest child is the most likely to be pampered or "spoiled" in Adler's view. Pampering prevents the child from learning what it is like to struggle against life's challenges and experience personal success. As a result, the child may come to lack mastery experiences, which then makes it difficult or impossible to feel independent in life. For Adler, the situation of a pampered youngest child creates an overinflated sense of ambitiousness that is made impotent by confidence problems and laziness. It is important to keep in mind, however, that none of this is certain. The ongoing dynamics of the child's interpersonal relationships and the influence of creative power in the formation of a personality make it impossible to predict developmental outcomes such as these in the abstract.

Final Remarks

Alfred Adler's individual psychology is anything but individualist in nature. Quite the contrary, it gives one a more empathically attuned understanding of the relational aspects of selfhood and goal setting in personality formation. While his ideas are very harmonious with those of William Stern and Gordon Allport, Adler's theory provides additional insights into the origins of personality. Adler drew from out of the infant's situation of relative inferiority the motivation to attach to others, grow, and achieve a unified lifestyle. If the individual can transition from being a near helpless child to an empowered adult with the assistance of her primary caretakers, her primary goal orientation will increasingly shift from overcoming inferiority to exploring the productive possibilities inherent to social interest. Adler highlights the intense degree to which the will and creative impetus of the person are interpersonally emergent. Selfhood is seen as "unbounded," embodied, and externalized, making personality thoroughly interactional on the whole. In Adler's view, personality formation is a function of dynamic exchanges between the forces of inheritance, physiology, social context, social position (including birth order), and creative power. Though rooted in causal antecedents, personality is simultaneously self-determined and future-oriented. The personality is to be understood in terms of motivated movement, social interface, joint meaning-making, and personal perception.

Suggested Readings

Adler, A. (1935). Introduction. *International Journal of Individual Psychology, 1,* 5-8.

Adler, A. (1958). *What life should mean to you.* New York, NY: Capricorn Books.

Adler, A. (1979). *Superiority and social interest.* New York, NY: Norton.

Adler, A. (1992). *Understanding human nature* (C. Brett, Trans.). Boston: Oneworld Publications.

Adler, A. (1998). *Social interest: Adler's key to the meaning of life.* Boston, MA: Oneworld.

DeRobertis, E. M. (2012). *The whole child: Selected papers on existential-humanistic child psychology.* Charleston, SC: CreateSpace Publishing.

Weber, D. A. (2003). A comparison of individual psychology and attachment theory. *Journal of Individual Psychology, 59,* 246-262.

Chapter 9
Karen Horney and Carl Rogers:
The Realizing-Actualizing Personality

This chapter focuses on the ideas of Karen Horney and Carl R. Rogers. Horney is known as a psychoanalytic thinker while Rogers is known as one of the founders of humanistic psychology. Nonetheless, there is extensive overlap between Horney's and Rogers's views of personality. The holistic, social psychological emphasis of Horney's work makes her theory decidedly humanistic. Thus, Horney experts often note that Horney's mature theory is most similar to the kinds of viewpoints espoused by humanists. Conversely, Rogers cited Horney's ideas concerning the self-realization process as being similar to his understanding of the self-actualizing tendency.

This chapter takes up the theme of selfhood that has been developing throughout recent chapters. With William Stern and Gordon Allport, the self was identified with those aspects of the personality experienced as warm or otherwise personally relevant and value-laden. The self was most closely affiliated with the synthetic unification or integration of the total personality. In addition, selfhood was seen as intimately connected to goal setting. These themes were present in Alfred Adler's personality theory as well, with Adler emphasizing the co-creative aspects of goal setting as a means toward the consolidation of a unified lifestyle. Adler identified numerous factors involved in stirring the individual's creative power into action, including inheritance, embodiment, self-movement, social position, cooperative social relations, feelings of incompleteness or inferiority, imagination, perception, and cooperative meaning-making.

With this chapter, Karen Horney and Carl Rogers will introduce yet another significant dimension of selfhood. Namely, Horney and Rogers give one an appreciation of the extent to which the self *as represented to oneself and others* matches or mirrors the individual's actual experience and innermost desires for being in the world with others. Horney and Rogers both addressed the realness, trueness, genuineness, or wholeheartedness of the personality. To accomplish this task required reviving a distinction made famous by William James between one's actual self-concept and one's ideal self-concept. To state the matter negatively, Horney and Rogers addressed the human capacity for self-alienation in personality formation.

Karen Horney

Horney's reputation as a humanistic analyst stems in no small measure from her holistic orientation, which is exemplified by her emphasis on self-development. For Horney, selfhood is a holistic notion that is incompatible with the Freudian subdivided personality. Horney rejected the mechanistic, reductionistic view of personality presented in Freud's psychosexual theory. Horney's self does not refer to any kind of psychic apparatus like an id or ego, nor is her self a homunculus. According to Horney, the *real self* is the always-unique inner force of growth in each human being. Being one's real self means realizing one's particular talents and living in accord with one's individuality within a context of fulfilling interpersonal relationships. Whereas Freud's depiction of personality revolved around the ego's constant efforts to manage conflict, Horney saw the personality governed by the real self as integrated and at peace. The self is integrative and growth oriented, and this contrasts with Freudian theory, which is focused on conflict and the past.

Like Freud and Alder, Horney saw personality formation as rooted in a theory of child development. According to Horney, a child's relationships with her primary caretakers powerfully influence whether or not the real self will emerge during the course of personality development. A child's family is the most important aspect of her developmental milieu. This does not mean that early childhood development is the exclusive determining force in personality formation. Horney considered development to be rooted in a set of intrinsic potentialities. Horney did not consider the evolution of selfhood to be a learned process in the manner of behaviorism. In her view, human beings are born with an innate drive to realize the true self, a process that she referred to as *self-realization*. Moreover, though development prior to the adolescent transition into adulthood is potent and highly influential, it does not preclude the development of freewill except under highly adverse circumstances.

Horney held that adequate parenting allows self-realization to proceed unimpeded. A health-conducive parental relationship is one that provides the child with proper parental love. Her belief concerning personality development is that the real self naturally emerges as an inherent part of human nature if the individual is allowed to grow and mature in an uncorrupted manner. In particular, Horney held that, as a child, the person must have been accepted, embraced, and permitted to grow according to her individual needs and possibilities. Parents need to empathize with and understand the child as the particular individual she is. Empathy must be communicated to the child via genuine warmth and interest. The result of this loving warmth is that the growing individual will develop a deep and validating sense of belonging, or what Horney called *we-ness*. This sense of belonging, in turn, will bring out *basic confidence*. The person is emboldened by her nuturant social milieu, given a fundamental sense of adequacy and self-worth. These feelings of self-assuredness thereby stimulate the development of various positive, growth facilitating qualities that Horney identified as hallmarks of self-realization. These qualities are listed below.

- Being in touch with one's own wishes and desires
- Responsibility for one's thoughts, feelings, and actions
- A sense of vitality or "feeling alive"
- Accepting and embracing one's uniqueness
- A sense of belonging or "we-ness"
- Basic confidence in one's adequacy and value as a person
- Clarity and understanding with regard to one's feelings, thoughts, wishes, and interests
- The ability to tap resources and exercise will power
- The ability to actualize one's special capacities or gifts
- The ability to relate to others
- The ability to find one's set of values and aims in life
- Spontaneity of feeling and expression with others
- The ability to recognize one's limitations
- The ability to live in truth with oneself and others
- The ability to be oneself when alone and when with others
- Experiencing a feeling of evolution in one's personal development

Just as proper parental love facilitates a burgeoning self-realization process, inadequate parenting increases the potential for poor self-development. According to Horney, primary caretakers may truncate their child's self-development if they are unable or unwilling to somehow communicate loving affection and thereby emotionally bond with their child. The styles of behavior that constitute inadequate parenting are manifold for Horney. She believed that there were countless ways for parents to create an unsupportive, unhealthy childrearing environment. References to the varieties of behavior that would threaten a child's self development are strewn throughout Horney's works. For Horney, however, a particular parental behavior in and of itself may not necessarily constitute inadequate parenting. Rather, the more essential issue is the spirit in which parents care for the child and, correlatively, the way the child perceives her parents' attitudes toward her. In other words, the total affective atmosphere or emotional tone of the parent-child relationship ultimately determines the adequacy of parenting. Horney associated certain kinds of behavior with inadequate parenting if these behaviors would block the child from attaining the fundamental warmth and security needed for self-realization. The danger, Horney felt, was that the child would perceive a *lurking hypocrisy* in the environment, by which she meant that that the child would see her parents' love as nothing more than pretense.

When the child does not feel adequately loved, the immediate result is that she feels helpless and conceives the world as potentially menacing. She feels alone in a hostile environment. We-ness is replaced by insecurity and hostility. Feelings of isolation and vulnerability create a desperate situation for the child, a basic lack of self-confidence. Horney called this fundamental lack of confidence *basic anxiety* and noted that in order to manage it, the child finds herself forced to abandon the development of her real self. Lacking genuine warmth and interest, the child develops a feeling of not being valuable unless she is something she is *not*. In other words, if really being herself results in basic anxiety, then the only viable alternative to quell her fears of abandonment is to *avoid* her real self. The individual feels that in order to be wanted and loved she must uphold some kind of *image of acceptability*, something that she feels others would expect her to be. As a result, she gradually loses the "real me." Her genuine will, wishes, feeling, likes, and dislikes become paralyzed in fear. She gradually loses the capacity to fully comprehend her own values and becomes reliant on appearing acceptable according to the real or imagined views of others.

Thus, a parental relationship that arouses basic anxiety derails the individual's self-realization process. The real self is rejected and a schism occurs in the personality. Once the real self has been abandoned, Horney observed that various coping strategies are adopted in an attempt to overcome one's fundamental sense of insecurity. In Horney's view, any particular attempt to manage basic anxiety can be classified as either a *moving toward, moving against,* or *moving away* strategy. The anxious person will develop a passive and dependent interpersonal style (i.e., moving toward), an aggressive and dominant interpersonal style (i.e., moving against), or a withdrawn and isolative interpersonal style (i.e., moving away). Each mode of comportment promises to help the person manage her deep-seated fears of abandonment and rejection. To be sure, these strategies are not adopted consciously and with full intension. They are desperate, "automatic" reactions to an unbearably painful and difficult relationship with one's primary caretakers and oneself. These coping strategies are thus defensively and tenaciously guarded.

Since the three basic coping strategies are mutually exclusive in style, Horney also noted that one style must be chosen as a predominant behavioral trend as a substitute for genuine personality integration. Thus, the anxious person will come to rely on one of the three styles more than the others. Moreover, the person will find that she can strengthen her defenses against her feelings of insecurity by creating an *idealized image* of herself in her moving toward, against, or away from others. Consequently, she will lift herself above others by forming an aggrandized mental representation of her particular mode of flight from the painful feeling of insignificance and vulnerability. This idealization process involves a *self-glorification* that gives the individual a feeling of significance and superiority over others. According to Horney, compliance is reinterpreted as goodness, love, and saintliness. Aggressiveness is reinterpreted as strength, leadership, heroism, and omnipotence. Aloofness is reinterpreted to be wisdom, self-sufficiency, and independence.

Upholding a glorified image of oneself is, for Horney, a way for the person to prevent herself from being crippled by the feeling of being "thoroughly bad." Rigorously identifying oneself with a glorified, idealized self-image, promises to compensate for the depletion of the real self. Horney referred to the drive to actualize the perfectionistic goals of the idealized self as a *search for glory*, which exists in opposition to the genuine strivings of self-realization. Rather than developing the characteristics of the real self, Horney noted that the individual searching for glory is compulsively preoccupied with appearing perfectly aligned with her particular (impossible) "solution" to basic anxiety. The fantasy of perfection creates egocentrism and a sense of entitlement on the whole. That this perfection is merely self-deception is evidenced by the prevalence of self-hate and hypersensitivity in the personality. The person's defensiveness is indicative of the fundamental conflicts of her psychological life. These include her contradictory attitudes toward others and the rift between her idealized self and the hated real self, which is tied to basic anxiety and feelings of worthlessness.

Carl Rogers

Carl Rogers also examined personality development in a holistic fashion. Rather than making psychological constructs such as the id or ego the focus of his observations, Rogers sought an empirically verifiable theory of the whole person. Rogers tended to use the terms *organism* and *person* interchangeably. However, the term *organism* was preferred term when he referred specifically to "sensory and visceral equipment." The term *person* was favored when Rogers referred to the one's mental capacities, one's phenomenal field of experience, one's self-concept, and one's self-ideal (i.e., the more psychological dimension of existence). This is not to imply that the person exists in isolation from the world with others. There is no possibility of a sharp limit between organism/person and environment.

According to Rogers, the developing personality has a single sovereign motivational predisposition, which he called *the actualizing tendency*. The actualizing tendency is the innate tendency of the personality to develop all of its biological and psychological capacities in ways that serve to maintain or enhance itself. The actualizing tendency is present at birth and observable in infancy.

As infancy progresses and the child begins to experience more and more of a sense of autonomy and control over her body and surroundings, she starts to develop what Rogers called a dawning awareness of "I experience." At this time, a particularly significant dimension of the organism becomes manifest, which Rogers referred to as the experience of selfhood or *the self*. As Rogers noted, a major aspect of the actualizing tendency is the capacity of the individual, *in a growth-promoting environment*, to move toward self-understanding and self-direction.

Rogers's self is not a homunculus either. As was the case with Horney, the self is but one expression of the general tendency of the personality to behave in those ways which maintain and enhance itself. The self is not the total organism either, but is rather the awareness of being, of functioning. The self and the self-concept tend to be interchangeable terms for Rogers. For Rogers, the self is an organized, fluid, but consistent conceptual pattern of perceptions, characteristics, relationships, and values referring back to the "I" or the "me." This is not to say that the self always remains within *focal* or *conscious* awareness. For Rogers, the self is more precisely merely *available* to awareness. The self is a fluid and changing *Gestalt*, a dynamic system.

As the self-concept evolves, the infant arrives at increasingly sophisticated understandings of herself in relation to others and her environment. This process is value laden, meaning that the child begins to see certain kinds of worldly and interpersonal relations as good, neutral, or bad. Under healthy circumstances, the child is allowed to positively value experiences that she perceives as enhancing her life and negatively value experiences that appear to threaten her development. Here, the self is said to be congruent with the genuine aims of the whole person or organism. As a result, a complementary *self-actualizing tendency* begins to develop in consort with the global actualizing tendency.

Whether or not the child develops a healthy self-actualizing tendency in the direction of a *genuine* self-ideal has to do with the nature of her upbringing, especially her interactions with her primary caretakers. When the child is old enough to comprehend parental judgments such as "good" or "bad," these social experiences are directly related to her self-concept. Healthy developmental conditions are those in which the child experiences unconditionally caring parental affection (i.e., *unconditional positive regard*). The result of these conditions is that the individual will most likely view herself as good, as worthy of love. Unconditional positive regard refers to the genuine affirmation of a person's intrinsic value as a unique individual. It does not altogether preclude a parent disapproving of "naughty" behaviors, for example. Rather, what it communicates to the developing person is that she never has to question whether or not she is truly loved and accepted for being herself. The developing person who has been given unconditional positive regard will have an unwavering faith that she is an inherently worthwhile and loveable creature. She can experience *fully* and accept herself. The person who was not threatened by the loss of love can be open to the full range of her organismic experiences.

The personality that would result from unconditional positive regard would be realistic, based upon an accurate symbolization of all the evidence given by the individual's sensory and visceral equipment. Thus, the self-structure of healthy developing individuals is integrated, whole, and genuine. This experientially open, *congruent self* actualizes its potentials in consort with its more global actualizing tendency in the direction of a particular self-ideal or *ideal self*. In Rogers's theory, *ideal self* is a term used to denote the self-concept that the individual would most like to possess, upon which she places the highest value for herself. These individuals can let the flow of their experience carry them in a forward-moving direction toward tentative goals and ideals. Moreover, when the actualizing tendency of the organism is adopted by the self, the self-actualizing tendency orients the person's development in the direction of socialization, broadly defined. The self both develops in an interpersonal context and desires good interpersonal relations during the growth process. Rogers observed that the actualizing self has numerous qualities, such as those listed below.

- Down-to-earth, realistic, perceptions and judgments are grounded in facts
- Open to experience without feeling threatened or being defensive

- Mature and responsible, owns one's feelings
- Accepts others as unique individuals
- Accepts and prizes oneself unconditionally
- Accepts and prizes others for who they are
- Has an internal locus of evaluation when judging oneself
- Willingness to be "in process," tolerance of change and ambiguity
- Appreciation of the uniqueness of each moment of one's life
- Experience of oneself as "fully functioning," general sense of richness of one's life experience
- Spontaneity, displays unpredictable creativity
- Trusts oneself, confidence in one's skills, perceptions, and evaluations
- Displays a life-affirming nurturance of all living things
- Open, expressive, flexible, and willing to take risks in relationships
- Independent, autonomous, self-motivated to seek fulfillment
- Seeks enhancement over the maintenance of one's organism overall

When the child is *not* given unconditional positive regard, however, healthy self-development is jeopardized. For instance, should the child experience her parents as disapproving of certain behaviors that she enjoys or would otherwise value positively, she may (depending on the spirit of the parenting) perceive her parents as saying, "You are bad and you are not loveable when you behave this way." This threatens her self-worth, her feeling of lovability as a person. There is, in Rogers's view, no greater threat to development. For this reason, the individual will take measures to survive this threatening situation. In particular, she will deny and/or distort her organismic experience. In order to guard against losing the sense of being loved, the individual finds herself compelled to refashion her phenomenal field of experience to fit what she perceives her parents as wanting in exchange for their love. The individual warps her experience in order to conceive of herself as a certain kind of person for the purposes of being perceived as "acceptable." Consequently, the values inherent to the personality are in some instances real, but are in other instances false. The personality comes to revolve around *conditions of worth* as a result of *conditional* positive regard from one's primary caretakers.

As the process of denying and distorting one's genuine experience proceeds, the self-concept becomes increasingly alienated from the total organism. Accurate representations of experience are not allowed to be made conscious. Experiences other than those that meet the personality's conditions of worth cause the individual anxiety because such experience threaten her feeling of value and lovability. Instead of developing a healthy, maturing, congruent self, the individual with conditions of worth manifests an *incongruent self* that is at variance with her organismic experience. A rift occurs between the actualizing tendency and the self-actualizing tendency. Self-actualization is no longer genuine, but rather false and disconnected from the person's real feelings and desires. The individual's distorted self-concept prevents optimal functioning.

Rogers noted that this self-concept could exclude either positive or negative evaluations. That is, individuals may deny that they have a good or bad trait in order to preserve a distorted self-image. However, the general point is, incongruence creates a situation wherein the personality comes to be patterned in accord with false ideals. Real self-actualization is stunted or thwarted. Incongruence creates inner tension. The self becomes defensive, rigid, socially maladjusted, and confused with regard to its own motives, feelings, and behaviors. Behavior is intellectually regarded as enhancing the self when no such value is directly experienced. Behavior is intellectually regarded as *opposed* to the enhancement of the self when there is no direct *negative* experience to corroborate this belief. In the end, the person is left with a distorted sense of self and a poor self-image. This increases the likelihood that she will display insecurity in relationships with others.

Final Remarks

Karen Horney and Carl Rogers add depth and detail to an understanding of how selfhood emerges from within the mother-child relationship. They alert one to the fact that qualities like warmth, empathy, genuine acceptance, and an overall spirit of unconditional positive regard (not to be confused with pampering or over-indulgence) are critical in assuring the genuineness and structural integrity of the personality. Horney and Rogers both recapitulate the idea mentioned in reference to Erik Erikson's ego-psychological perspective, that the mother needs to have a deep belief in the meaning of her parenting behaviors. In addition to merely "providing for" the child's physiological needs, the mother must carry herself with an air of welcoming receptivity for the purpose of establishing an abiding emotional bond with her child. This bond provides the confidence and sense of value or self-worth that founds healthy personality development and social adjustment.

Horney and Rogers bring into focus the ways in which selfhood is a *growth-oriented* dimension of the personality, one that emerges from nurturant social relations. They each provided relevant data concerning how self-development can facilitate the formation of a personality with qualities like emotional stability, wholeheartedness, and overall vitality. Horney and Rogers provide a much needed distinction between those instances when the self is being realized and actualized in accord with genuine desires and when the self is sent on a wild goose chase after a falsified, idealized self. That is, they make an important distinction between the genuine article and the imitation when it comes to personality.

Suggested Readings

Barton, A. (1974). *Three worlds of therapy: Freud, Jung, & Rogers.* Palo Alto, CA: National Press Books.

DeRobertis, E. M. (2008). *Humanizing child developmental theory: A holistic approach.* New York: iUniverse.

Horney, K. (1937). *The neurotic personality of our time.* NY: W. W. Norton.

Horney, K. (1939). *New ways in psychoanalysis.* NY: W. W. Norton.

Horney, K. (1945). *Our inner conflicts: a constructive theory of neurosis.* NY: W. W. Norton.

Horney, K. (1950). *Neurosis and human growth: the struggle toward self-realization.* NY: W. W. Norton.

Rogers, C. R. (1951). *Client-centered therapy: Its current practice, implications and theory.* Boston: Houghton Mifflin.

Rogers, C. R. (1959). A theory of therapy, personality, and interpersonal relationships, as developed in the client-centered framework. In S. Koch (Ed.), *Psychology: A study of a science (Vol. 3)* (184–256). NY: McGraw Hill.

Rogers, C. R. (1961). *On becoming a person: A therapist's view of psychotherapy*. Boston: Houghton Mifflin.

Rogers, C. R. (1980). *A way of being*. Boston: Houghton Mifflin.

Chapter 10
Abraham Maslow
and Viktor Frankl:
The Transcending-Actualizing
Personality

Abraham Maslow and Viktor Frankl come from two different branches of the third force, humanistic, or human science movement in psychology. Maslow is a founder of the specifically American branch of humanistic psychology, while Frankl comes from the tradition of European existential psychology. In fact, Frankl has on certain occasions questioned whether or not he should be affiliated with the mainstream of humanistic psychology due to differences in theoretical emphasis. Nonetheless, I have deemed it appropriate to bring them together for the current chapter for two reasons. First, Frankl's work has more in common with the breadth of ideas emanating from humanistic psychology than any other tradition of thought. One reason for this is that the perspectives inherent to humanistic psychology are intensely diverse. Second, Frankl's hesitations about being affiliated with humanistic psychology tend to revolve around his emphasis on the notion of *self-transcendence*, which he felt was underrepresented in most humanistic theories. However, Abraham Maslow secured a place for transcending self-actualizers in his mature theory. This chapter presents ideas from Maslow and Frankl in order to introduce the reader to the transcending personality, which will act as a point of departure for the last section of this text (i.e., *nested* interpersonal personality theorizing).

Abraham Maslow

Abraham Maslow created his personality theory by drawing upon three currents of thought: Gestalt psychology, functionalism (e.g., William James), and psychoanalysis (e.g., Freud and Adler). From Gestalt psychology and functionalism Maslow derived the idea that a human being cannot be reduced to a collection of individual parts. The person's various organs, inclinations, and psychological capacities all work together to form a functional whole. From psychoanalysis, Maslow took the idea that the functioning of the organism is complex, involving a wide variety of interactions between mind and body that are continuous, yet not always consciously understood. As a result, Maslow called his theory a *holistic-dynamic theory*.

Maslow's personality theory is grounded in a theory of motivation. Like Allport, Maslow held that the behavior of an individual has many determinants, and cannot be understood on the basis of a single motive. Behavior may spring from many motives, as anyone who has been on a date knows. Something as simple as eating a meal can be a social affair as well as a biochemical affair. Moreover, Maslow proposed that the motives that govern the formation of a personality are rooted in a *hierarchy of needs*.

Human beings have a number of needs, but these needs make themselves known to the individual from within a prioritized motivational framework. This is not a theory of child development, nor is it a "stage" theory. Rather, for Maslow, certain needs tend to have a global or generalized priority over others in personality functioning. When a need is satisfied, it loses its status as the primary motive and gives way to a new motive that tends to take precedence over the others. Satisfactions generate new motivations, but the needs that comprise the hierarchy do not go away. Well satisfied needs simply become less potent motivational forces in the personality.

In Maslow's view, there are certain needs that must be met if a human being is to be free of pathology. He called these *deficiency needs* or "basic" needs. All people everywhere share these deficiency needs. Therefore, Maslow made them the first needs on the hierarchy. Human deficiency needs consist of *physiological needs, safety needs, love and belongingness needs, and esteem needs* respectively. Physiological needs are needs for food, water, oxygen, and so forth. Without the means to satisfy these needs, the organism would die. Once these needs are met, the person will then become interested in securing their safety. The person will be motivated to seek a stable, secure environment in which to live. Once accomplished, the personality will then become dominated by the desire for intimacy with other human beings, affiliation and affection. Having achieved a sense of love and belonging from others, the individual will then seek to realize her intrinsic value as person through accomplishments, achievements, and other demonstrations of competence. With the satisfaction of esteem needs, Maslow believed the individual will have avoided any serious threats to her health. In addition, the satisfaction of esteem needs readies the personality for the potential satisfaction of *self-actualization needs*.

However, when deficiency needs are not met, they lead to the development of neurotic needs. Neurotic needs are compensatory impulses rooted in the lack of satisfaction of normal human needs. So, for example, a person who has not had her safety needs met might find herself compelled to pursue goals designed to compensate for feelings of insecurity. A person who has not had her belongingness needs met might find herself compelled to pursue goals designed to compensate for feelings of isolation and loneliness. There is no obvious limit to the ways in which these compensatory behaviors might manifest themselves.

Self-actualization needs are not needs such as what has been discussed thus far in that unsatisfied self-actualization needs will not result in neurotic needs. It is more the case that the person will simply not be as fulfilled in life as she could be. Maslow referred to self-actualization needs as *meta-needs*, indicating a striving or desire to fulfill ideals perceived to be valuable to one's very *being* (one's unique personality) rather than a "need" in the ordinary sense. This level of the hierarchy is not like the others and does not follow the same rules. It is not as neat and orderly. Rather, it is highly individualized. Meta-needs are also referred to as *being-values* or *B-values*. Below is a list of fourteen common B-values.

1. Autonomy
2. Truth
3. Beauty
4. Goodness
5. Wholeness
6. Aliveness
7. Uniqueness
8. Perfection
9. Completion

10. Justice
11. Simplicity
12. Totality
13. Effortlessness
14. Humor

As you might imagine, not all optimally functioning, thriving individuals would be equally invested in each B-value. Some might be held in higher esteem than others, depending on the self-actualizing person in question. Meta-needs are the most autonomous of all the needs and they are the least stereotyped. Moreover, they lead to the greatest happiness.

According to Maslow, there are various traits that are more common among self-actualizing people than non-self-actualizing people. Fifteen of the traits identified by Maslow are broken down below under their typical category headings comprised of awareness, honesty, freedom, and trust.

Awareness
1. Penetrating perception of reality
2. Freshness of appreciation (wonder, awe)
3. Higher likelihood of intense "peak experiences" of fulfillment
4. The ability to discriminate between means and ends

Honesty
5. Social interest (as described by Alfred Adler)
6. Humility, and respect, ethics (profound interpersonal relations)
7. Democratic character
8. A non-hostile sense of humor

Freedom
9. Spontaneity
10. Need for solitude
11. Autonomy
12. Creativity

Trust

13. Acceptance of self, others, and nature
14. Problem-centeredness (rather than ego-centered)
15. Resistance to blind enculturation

It is important to note, however, that self-actualization is not universally pursued. It is equally important to note that Maslow's theory is not a trait theory. Self-actualization is not the mere accumulation of the above characteristics. Self-actualization is a lifestyle, a perpetual work in progress, and not an end state. A personality can never be said to be self-actualized "once and for all," so to speak. Self-actualization entails living life to one's full potential, being oneself, and pursuing one's ideals irrespective of what anyone else expects or demands. Self-actualizing people have an insatiable appetite for life, for learning, and for becoming exactly who they feel they ought to become. While this may sound appealing, Maslow believed that it is not easy to come by. Throughout life people are faced with family expectations, peer pressure, and societal demands to conform and obey. Achieving great things is often met with jealously even by people once thought to be friends. Thus, people do not "automatically" move on to the last level of the hierarchy.

Though unmet meta-needs (i.e., unfulfilled B-values) do not result in the emergence of neurotic needs, they are not necessarily without consequences. Unmet meta-needs can result in *meta-pathology* or emotional distress resulting from the absence of meaning and fulfillment in life. One form of meta-pathology is called the *Jonah Complex* or the evasion of growth. This represents the fear of being one's best, if for no other reason than the envy, jealousy, and hostility one encounters from others when living life to one's fullest potential. The Jonah complex can also be elicited by the fear of the intense emotionality (e.g., the ecstatic joy) that comes along with being one's best. Another form of meta-pathology is *desacralization*, which refers to the loss of a sense of the important, the precious, and the special due to a deep sense of social disillusionment and a pervasive mistrust of values and virtues.

Having realized that it can be difficult to lead a self-actualizing lifestyle, Maslow specified certain ways that people move toward embracing B-values and addressing their meta-needs. What follows is a sample of these transitional phenomena.

- Experiencing things, events, situations, and others with full-absorption, vividly, and selflessly
- Choosing growth opportunities rather than habitually opting for adaptive functioning or maintaining present securities
- Becoming self-aware
- Being honest
- Learning to trust one's judgment and in one's ability to make good life choices
- Working at doing things with excellence and mastery
- Abandoning and avoiding egoic defensiveness
- Relishing in (rather than retreating from) *peak* and *plateau* experiences.

Of the items presented above, *peak* and *plateau* experiences have special import for Maslow's mature theory of personality.

Peak experiences are "moments" of self-actualization wherein the person feels more whole, more integrated, and more aware of herself and the world. She experiences unprecedented clarity of thought and feeling as well as a loving acceptance of others. These periods can be highly constructive and highly creative as well. Plateau experiences are similar to peaks moments, but have a more enduring character, as if the person has learned to live life in general in the aura of "the transcendent vision" characteristic of the peak experience. The reader versed in mystical or Eastern spiritual traditions will likely find the language of peak and plateau experiences vaguely familiar. With these insights, Maslow was pointing to the possibility of a future psychology called *fourth force* or *transpersonal* psychology designed to handle the self-transcendent, spiritual aspects of human psychology. Transpersonal experiences are those wherein an individual's sense of self extends beyond the individual and integrates with a wider, supra-personal reality. Since some self-actualizing individual's appear to be more open to transpersonal experience than others, Maslow made a distinction between pragmatic self-actualizers and transcending self-actualizers. The latter group, he believed, had a more profound sense of humility and a deeper appreciation for the sacred, the ambiguous, the awe-inspiring, and the mystical or transcendental.

Viktor E. Frankl

Viktor E. Frankl was an Austrian psychoanalytic psychiatrist who came under the influence of two currents of thought that originated in philosophy: existentialism and phenomenology. *Existentialism* began as a reaction against what was perceived to be a pervasive bias toward abstract, hyper-rational thinking in Western culture. Søren Kierkegaard, who is thought to be a founder of the movement, insisted that philosophers and scientists should focus more of their efforts on understanding those things that matter the most to human beings: their decisions in life. From an existential point of view, life is in large part a series of impassioned decisions that a person must make. *Phenomenology*, in Frankl's works, refers to a qualitative method of data collection that was created by the German philosopher Edmund Husserl. A phenomenological approach to research in psychology involves inquiring as to the *quality* and *meaning* of human behavior as experienced first-hand by the individuals under study. A phenomenologist would not begin research on depression, for instance, by making the assumption that the condition is nothing but the side-effect of an anonymous biochemical irregularity. Rather, a phenomenological approach to data collection would begin by asking *what it is* that "being depressed" means to the depressed person forced to cope with the condition on a day-to-day basis.

Frankl ingeniously combined these two traditions of thought by creating an approach to personality that focuses on the uniquely human search for meaning-in-life. Frankl joined the existential focus on life decisions and the phenomenological focus on meaning to create a view of personality that envisions human beings as creatures who thrive on discovering opportunities for creating a meaningful existence. Thus, the relative freedom of the will, responsibility, commitment, and purpose all play a central role in Frankl's thought.

According to Frankl, personality development is stratified, with formative influences emanating from at least four different points of origin. As a psychiatrist, Frankl held there are *endogenic* factors (meaning forces "from within" a system) involved in personality formation, referring to the kinds of life influences discussed in genetics, biology, anatomy and physiology, endocrinology, biochemistry, and so forth. As a psychiatrist trained in Freudian and Adlerian versions of psychoanalysis, Frankl also held that personality is subject to the influences of *psychogenic* and *sociogenic* forces as well. Psychogenic factors are those most commonly studied and discussed in the context of developmentally oriented psychology and the psychology of individual functioning in general, while sociogenic factors are those most closely associated with social psychological, sociological, and cultural-anthropological research. For Frankl, the fourth set of formative life influences comes from the mind of the individual herself, envisioned as irreducible to all of the other elements of the personality system. This resulted from his philosophical training in existential-phenomenology. Here, Frankl spoke of a *noögenic* aspect of the personality. The individual human being is a creative influence *in her own right* in the unfolding of her personality formation, particularly by way of the fact that interpretive meaning-making is required for personality formation. Frankl referred to this as the "spiritual" aspect of personality, which he considered to be a dimension of personal meaning. The endogenic, psychogenic, sociogenic, and noögenic aspects of the personality form an integrative system or *Gestalt* along the lines of William Stern's *unitas multiplex*, with no element being fully reducible to another.

Like Maslow, Frankl's approach to personality is rooted in a theory of motivation. Individual personalities may be more or less mature depending on the motives that characteristically underlie their decision-making and life goals. According to Frankl, human beings seek to satisfy three kinds of motives in life: the will-to-pleasure, the will-to-power, and the *will-to-meaning*. As Freud, Skinner, and many other psychologists have noted numerous times, human beings seem to be naturally drawn toward the attainment of physical pleasure. Inasmuch as this plays a formative role in the development of a personality, Frankl referred to this as a person's will-to-pleasure. In addition, human beings want to feel empowered in life. They want to feel competent, strong, and independent. Hence, a young child might exclaim, "I'm three *and a half*," while an adolescent might try cigarettes in order to look more mature. This is the person's will-to-power at work. However, for Frankl, personality development need not stop here. Frankl considered a genuinely mature, optimally functioning, and resilient personality to be motivated by the will-to-meaning, which he considered to be a self-*transcending* tendency. People motivated by the will-to-meaning are not focused on attaining pleasure or power for themselves. Rather, their primary aim is to devote themselves to the welfare of something or someone *outside* themselves (something akin to William Stern's *heterotelie*, but with more emphasis on the dimension of life meaning). Self-transcendence is thus a value-rich orientation toward life.

Frankl's approach to personality reminds us that we all need a reason to get up in the morning and persevere through the hard times. He considered the will-to-meaning to be a wellspring of strength in the face of adversity. People are capable of enduring unimaginable suffering, Frankl noted, when they believe that the suffering has a meaning or value. In fact, it was partially due to his contact with Frankl that Maslow began to increasingly include an emphasis on transcending motives in his characterizations of self-actualizing people.

At the same time, it is worthwhile to note that Viktor Frankl added a measure of controversy to the humanistic movement with his particular introduction of a self-transcendent will-to-meaning in personality. Viktor Frankl was once a prisoner of war and spent time is Nazi concentration camps. During his time in the camps, Frankl observed that there were people who crumbled like a Maslowian house of cards upon the denial of their basic needs. The personalities of these individuals seemed to be driven by lower, deficiency needs in day-to-day behavior. At the same time, however, Frankl insisted that there were people in the camps who were able to tap into strengths that they would have never discovered about themselves were it not for the adversity that they had come to endure. These individual's (and he counted himself among them) did not seem to move down the hierarchy, nor did he feel that they merely stayed steadfast at a self-actualized level or even moved up to one. Rather, Frankl believed that there was a *different kind* of motive that strengthened these individuals and provided resistance to their adversity, a motive that was not properly emphasized in the standard account of Maslow's hierarchy. Frankl considered this motive to be the self-transcendent will-to-meaning. People who were able to focus their attention on a commitment to something or someone *other than themselves*, something or someone meaningful that needed their devotion, were provided a reason to persevere. Frankl had much faith in the possibility of appealing to a person in a meaning-focused cognitive manner to make alterations in a personality structure, potentially making the hierarchy inapplicable in any given circumstance. Thus, he was not an advocate of the strictness or necessity of the hierarchy.

In Maslow's defense, Maslow's account of the self-actualization process was never devoid of a self-transcendent aspect, and as his theory matured it became increasingly pronounced. Moreover, Maslow did allow for occasional exceptions to his hierarchy. However, Frankl's criticisms had yet another aspect to them. Frankl insisted that self-actualization was not attainable in the way that humanistic psychologists tended to suggest, which he interpreted to be the result of a deliberate and focused effort. Frankl insisted that self-actualization is the result of a self-transcending orientation rather than "the other way around." Human potential is best tapped through an *outward focused* attention to things, others, events, situations, projects, and relationships that are perceived to be meaningful or valuable. To unlock potentials, one must be devoted to something *other than one's own self-actualization*. To be sure, this critique is open to question as well. Not all humanistic psychologists have characterized self-actualization and the self-actualization process the same way. Moreover, if one looks at Maslow's characterization of self-actualization, one will note that he was careful to emphasize things like social interest, problem-centeredness, acceptance of others, and the like.

In the end, this theoretical battle amounted to a lover's quarrel and a difference in emphasis at best. What is important to learn from this debate is that humanistic psychology is not a "self-centered" tradition of thought, as contemporary "positive" psychologists have suggested. Quite the contrary, Frankl saw the self-transcendent aspects of human personality as a guard against the dangers of subjectivism and pure relativism. As he noted, popular writers calling themselves existentialists sometimes neglect the relative objectivity of human meaning and value. These writers, he held, repeat *ad nauseam* that personality must be understood on the basis of being-in-the-world, but forget to mention that *meaning* is also in-the-world and is thus not a *merely* personal, *merely* subjective aspect of reality. Meaning is more than "just" self-expression or *a projection* of the self *on to* or *into* a world of dead matter, and this is a message that positive psychologists have yet to comprehend.

In recognizing the need to preserve the integrity and "otherness" of meaning in its own right, Frankl was sensitive to the call of responsibility that comes from respecting differences. As he put it, if meanings and values were just something emerging from a "subject" rather than something stemming from a sphere *beyond and above* the individual, then they would instantly lose their *demand quality*. This bears a direct relationship to the interpersonal, ethical, and moral aspects of personality formation. For Frankl, self-transcendence is equally implied whether a person transcends herself through general meaning fulfillment or loving encounter in particular. In the first case, a supra-personal meaning is implicated, whereas in loving encounter an expressly interpersonal meaning is fulfilled. Loving a person reveals her essential uniqueness, which is a core element of both personhood and personality according to Frankl.

Similar to Maslow, Frankl believed that there can be deleterious consequences for not satisfying "higher" human needs. If a person lacks or has lost a sense of meaning-in-life, this will give rise to what Frankl called *noögenic neurosis*. Noögenic neurosis is a term that Frankl used to refer to the emotional distress and dysfunction that result from a lack or loss of meaning-in-life (i.e., an unfulfilled will-to-meaning). For Frankl, the movement toward a self-transcending orientation is a natural process in human personality formation. When this tendency is blocked for some reason, a painful form of self-consciousness can result. This sort of self-consciousness can manifest itself in many forms, such as feelings of anxiety, chronic boredom, depressive states, compulsive behaviors, and so forth. In all instances, the individual is focused on their own discomfort rather than on the things and people around them that would otherwise bring happiness into their lives. For Frankl, this is the hidden meaning behind Freud's now famous claim that the aim of therapy is to return a person to their capacity for love and work. Thus, he devised a style of doing meaning-focused therapy called *logotherapy*, the aim of which was to help clients connect to a more self-transcendent lifestyle (Frankl translated the Greek word *logos* as "meaning").

In effect, whereas Maslow's version of self-transcendence was more or less connected to *exceptional* states of consciousness, Frankl saw self-transcendence as applicable to day-to-day living as well. When he referred to the search for life meanings embedded within the fabric of daily existence, Frankl spoke of a *secular logos*. When he referred to the search for "higher," more sacred or religious sorts of life meanings (i.e., something more akin to Maslow's peak experiences), Frankl spoke of an *eternal logos*.

Final Remarks

With Maslow and Frankl, personality theorizing becomes more motivationally informed. From Maslow, self-development and personality formation are motivated by physiological, safety, love and belongingness, esteem, and self-actualization needs. Frankl considered the will-to-pleasure to be roughly equivalent to what one finds in Freud's psychosexual theory, which would make it a parallel to Maslow's physiological needs. Frankl's will-to-power referred to the individual's striving for strength, competence, and self-enhancement, which is well-represented by Maslow's other needs, like safety, belonging, and esteem needs. Frankl's most original contribution came in the form of the self-transcendent will-to-meaning, which is unquestionably represented in Malsow's mature theory, but does not perfectly correspond to Maslow's transcending self-actualization. Maslow and Frankl each made original contributions to the notion of self-transcendence in human personality.

Maslow and Frankl leave the early developmental periods of human becoming and concentrate on the more advanced stages personality formation. In their respective emphases on the transcending-actualizing aspects of personality, both Maslow and Frankl highlight a realm of human existence that is highly paradoxical. The transcending-actualizing aspects of personality are the ultimate expressions of individuality, yet Maslow and Frankl also considered them to be universal needs among human beings. Thus, in the absence of their satisfaction, one is at risk for meta-pathology, to borrow Maslow's term.

With the introduction of the transcendent dimension in particular, Maslow and Frankl bring the transpersonal in personality formation into focus. The term *transpersonal* is being used here to refer to that which occurs through, across, and beyond the individual person. The individuality of the person is an illusion unto itself, as it is always a function of a wider contextual reality. This idea is already embedded within the architecture of the theories that have appeared in this section of the text, but it tended to remain focused on interpersonal relationships. By their transcendent orientations, Maslow and Frankl more readily move personality beyond the horizon of the interpersonal toward limitless vistas of meaningful world-relatedness. In effect, they have set the stage for a whole new array of discussions regarding the embedded, contextualized, or *nested* nature of personality. To say that something is nested means that it is a complex system operating within a still larger set of complex systems. The interpersonal relatedness of personality is a complex system operating within numerous other, wider complex systems.

Suggested Readings

Frankl, V. E. (1969). *The will to meaning: foundations and applications of logotherapy.* New York: Nal.

Frankl, V. E. (2006). *Man's search for meaning.* Boston: Beacon Press.

Maslow, A. H. (1970). *Motivation and personality.* New York: Longman.

Maslow, A. H. (1993). *The farther reaches of human nature.* New York: Penguin.

IV: NESTED INTERPERSONAL PERSONALITY THEORIZING

Chapter 11
Carl Jung: The Ancestrally Nested Personality

Next to Sigmund Freud, Carl Jung is arguably the most famous psychoanalyst who ever lived. Jung's school of thought is called *analytic psychology*. Like Alfred Alder, Jung believed humans to be motivated by both past events and future goals. In contrast to Freudian determinism, Jung maintained that humans constantly develop and achieve a more balanced, more complete form of personality. Unlike Freud, Jung was not a reductionist in his interpretation of the past or the unconscious. Themes revolving around unfulfilled desires and aggression do *not* have universal priority in the Jungian view of the unconscious. The unconscious may just as easily be seen as a great reservoir of untapped potential for growth.

Carl Jung created a personality theory that utilized some basic Freudian concepts, but he altered their meanings to suit his own viewpoint. The *ego*, for example, is a rational structure of the personality for Jung, just as it was for Freud. However, there is a stricter identification of the ego with the conscious mind in Jung's work. For Jung, the ego is the very center of the conscious mind. Phenomena like repression occur as the result of shifting *psychic energies* that change direction depending on the person's goals at any given time in life (rather than being a mere "ego defense," as it was for Freud). In other words, the ego is given a bit of a demotion in its managerial role when transitioning from Freudian to Jungian thought.

In Jung's work, the unconscious now has two meanings: there is a personal unconscious and a collective unconscious. The personal unconscious resides just below the conscious mind and occupies a place like Freud's preconscious mind. For Jung, there is more mutual interaction between the conscious and unconscious than Freud's theoretical formulations would lead us to believe. The personal unconscious houses what Jung called *complexes*. A complex is a dense cluster or node of emotionally charged images, ideas, values, and memories that occupies a somewhat larger than average "space" in the mind of the individual. A complex refers to any aspect of psychological functioning that has far reaching associations with the rest of one's psychology. Complexes color more of who a person is than other aspects of psychological life. So, for example, it would be quite natural for one's cognitive functioning to involve more connections to one's maternal relations than say one's favorite food. Jung would thus expect that a person would display a *mother complex* and that would be normal. In everyday language, we have become accustom to thinking that anything identified as a "complex" is pathological. This strict identification of complexes with pathology is not present in Jung's work, though he did believe it was possible for any complex to over-inflate in terms of its overall significance and take on a pathological character. In other words, it would be normal to have a mother complex. It would *not* be normal for one's mother complex to become so exaggerated that one's life decisions are habitually and compulsively tied to images of one's mother. Since complexes are in the personal unconscious, the person is typically only vaguely aware of their existence, but can become more aware of them with the right kind of effort or assistance.

For Jung, a complex can be the result of personal experiences. Thus, a person could have a pathological complex about the size of her nose from personal experiences of being teased at school. However, Jung believed that some complexes, like the aforementioned mother complex, are actually the combined result of personal experiences and *the collective experiences of many human beings over the course of our development as a species.* Any experience that is powerful and universal to being human is in contention for having created the prototype for a complex. Since all people everywhere have formed in the womb of a mother and been "mothered" by someone, it makes sense to Jung that there should be a mother complex. At this point, Jung asserted that there must be a level of unconscious functioning that is deeper and darker than Freud ever suspected. There must be a level of mental functioning that is tied to the collective experiences inherent to our evolutionary history, which Jung called the *collective unconscious.*

The collective unconscious houses the prototypes of species-wide complexes, which Jung called *archetypes.* An archetype is an archaic impression that is emotionally charged and liable to incite arousal, action, or forms of perception. They are powerful, implicit *racial memories*. Archetypes are archaic, emotionally charged "images" rooted in our ancestral past that predispose us to perceive and behave in more or less species-typical ways. The *core* contents (*not* the final product), thus, are similar for people in all cultures. An archetype is similar to an "instinct" or drive, but it is more psychological in nature, rather than biological. Archetypes are not innate ideas either, but rather innate tendencies to react holistically in a particular way to certain kinds of phenomena. They are responsible for the many myths, legends, and religious beliefs that human beings have created and represent the universal imagery that you find repeatedly reemerging in the great texts, political documents, movies, plays, and so forth. Staying with the example of one's mother, Jung believed that the intense joy or reverence that a person has for the image of her mother is not explained on the basis of personal experiences alone, but on the basis of the fact that throughout history people have experienced their mothers as protectors who can nonetheless punish, hurt, or destroy them. Accordingly, the age-old mother image or *great mother archetype* is a frequently appearing cultural symbol. Think of phrases such as "mother earth," "mother ship," and religious images of "the Madonna" and of goddesses and so forth.

At first these reaction patterns are not very vivid or clear, but over time, when they become associated with various iconic images (rather than just unreflective reactions), they then qualify as full-fledged "archetypes." Archetypes represent the common ground that psychologically binds us together as members of the same species. They are the basis of why humans can identify with each another in a deep and profound manner. Archetypes are the deepest aspects of the mind and the most difficult to comprehend. When a personal experience "corresponds" to an archaic, ancestral impression, the archetype is "activated." The archetype cannot be directly "represented" (i.e., symbolically, rationally), it can only be activated. This is not the stuff of logical discourse, which is the purview of the ego. Rather, archetypes express themselves most forcefully through dreams, fantasies, and delusions. Dreams were Jung's favorite hunting ground for archetypes. He found that, in dreams, we envision motifs that often coincide with scenes and ideas that were important to ancient peoples. Only a few archetypes have evolved to the point where they can be clearly conceptualized.

For Jung, archetypes often appear in opposing pairs, which represent opposing tendencies apparent in human functioning. So, for example, Jung considered the human psyche to have both a masculine and a feminine nature. This is universal and present throughout our evolutionary history as bisexual beings. Human beings have both masculine and feminine characteristics embedded within their biology (e.g., men still have nipples but produce no breast milk). Men and women have always had to relate to one another and achieve mutual understanding. Thus, Jung believed that there is a masculine aspect present in the female psyche, which he called the *animus*. Conversely, there is a feminine aspect within the male psyche, called the *anima*. The *animus* represents the rational, pragmatic tendency in humans, whereas the *anima* represents the more emotional, empathic, caring side of humans. His ideal vision of healthy human functioning involves striking a functional balance between these two tendencies. For instance, a male who represses and denies his feminine side altogether might be inordinately cold, possibly aggressive, yet deeply insecure about his sexuality. On the other hand, an over-identification with the feminine aspects of the psyche might make for an emotionally unstable male who may also display insecurities about gender or sexual identity. What the personality needs in both instances is moderation, balance, and thus, harmony. Below is a list of some of the other, more commonly identified archetypes.

- *Persona*: The profile of the personality that people show to the world, which tends to abide by social norms. The persona does not represent the whole personality and should not be mistaken for the self.
- *Shadow*: The deviant, "dark" side of the personality, which is more likely to be seen as morally objectionable. The shadow side of the personality can nonetheless house constructive and creative potentials that we might be reluctant to face.
- *Great Mother*: The archetype associated with both the positive and negative feelings related to mothering (i.e., both nourishment and the power of reprimand)

- *Wise Old Man (Senex)*: The striving for wisdom and meaning-in-life, the wise old man symbolizes our preexisting knowledge of the mysteries of life. Politicians and those who speak authoritatively in order to sound "sensible" and be influential try to access this archetype.
- *Puer Aeternus*: The eternal boy in us all.
- *Trickster*: Sometimes identified with the *Puer* archetype, the trickster represents the impulse to disobey rules and contradict conventional behavior. Since this can sometimes incite humor, the trickster can be depicted as a buffoon, jester, joker, or clown. The trickster can act as a catalyst for positive change or simply become a villain.
- *Hero*: The part of the personality that fights against the odds to vanquish an enemy of mankind and overcome darkness, evil, and so forth.

Because Jung saw such diversity within the human psyche, he believed that human health is dependent upon balance and harmony. Jung's emphasis on balance can be seen in his characterization of other personality structures, such as *character orientations* and *psychological functions*. Human personalities display two opposing character orientations: *introversion* and *extraversion*. Introverts have a bias to turn inward to one's own flow of experience, whereas extraverts tend to turn outward toward interactions with other people and the world at large. Psychological functions comprise two sets of opposites: *thinking* and *feeling*, *sensing* and *intuiting*. Thinkers rely on passionless intellectual analysis to adapt to the world, whereas feeling people tend to rely more heavily on emotionally colored conviction and value judgments. Sensing people adapt to their surroundings by relying on sense perception. They need to see it with their own eyes to believe it. Intuitive people go beyond what is present to the senses and rely on gut feelings or "hunches." In Jung's view, sensation tells you that something exists, thinking tells you what it is, feeling tells you whether it is agreeable, and intuition tells you both where it comes from and where it is going. Together, character orientations and psychological functions combine to make *psychological types* (for example, an introverted, thinking, intuitive person as contrasted with an extroverted, feeling, sensing person, and so forth).

Jung believed that each archetype, character orientation, and psychological function is capable of playing a growth-oriented role in human personality when acted upon in moderation. Since there are people who achieve a healthy, balanced lifestyle in the world, Jung needed to identify some aspect of the personality associated with the achievement of order. As is to be expected, he found the psychic tendency toward balance, moderation, and harmony in an archetype, which he called *the self*. The self is the innate tendency to move toward growth, balance, completion, and "perfection." The self stands in between the conscious and unconscious minds, as well as all the opposing extremes of the personality (e.g., anima-animus, introversion-extraversion, etc.). The self is symbolic of the wholesome and the hardy. It is the true core of the personality, not the ego. To achieve an understanding of this goes hand-in-hand with the development and subsequent harmonization of one's many opposing psychological tendencies. This is what Jung called *self-realization*, which is the ultimate goal of personality development. Self-realization depends upon an *individuation* process, whereby the various aspects of the personality (i.e., archetypes, character orientations, characteristic functions, life experiences in general) are fully developed. These, in turn, have to be synthesized over time into a well-functioning whole. This process of synthesis is referred to as *the transcendent function*. In other words, self-realization is dependent upon an unfolding dialectic of differentiation (i.e., individuation) and integration (i.e., the transcendent function).

The developmental character of self-realization prompted Jung to carve out various stages of the lifespan to compliment his personality theory. These stages include *childhood, youth, middle age*, and *old age*. Childhood is the time for coming into being. It is when the initial structuring of the ego emerges from the self. Youth is the time when the striving for independence appears. During youth, the individual is collecting up evidence to support the establishment of a belief system and characteristic lifestyle. Middle life is a time for crisis (since the lifespan is half over) and it is characterized by a need to revise one's personality along the lines of a deliberately conscious individuation process. If accomplished, individuation can lead to an unambiguous impetus toward harmonious synthesis and self-realization. Finally, old age is the time for reflection, the development of wisdom, and preparations for death.

Final Remarks

Carl Jung's personality theory situates personality within an evolutionary context, but not in a biologically reductive manner. Rather, Jung's approach to personality is quite holistic in emphasis and bears direct relevance to the psychological world of the person. For Jung, evolutionary history is born into the personality and maintained through the progression of cultures, their myths, their symbolism, their artistic forms of expression, and so forth. Jung gives one a sense of the sheer plurality inherent to personality and the vital need for balance, harmony, and integration for healthy human functioning.

Jung provides situational structure to the processes inherent to personality formation. The individual's experience and behavior are always nested within an ancestral past that always only manifests itself in specific cultural contexts. According to Jung's personality theory individual personalities are inextricably connected via the common threads embedded within the collective unconscious. The actualizing, realizing, and transcending tendencies of the self are still viewed as involving socially mediated processes of differentiation and synthesis, but are examined in an evolutionary and cultural light simultaneously.

By seeing personality as a function of a culturally endowed environmental context, Jung's theory calls attention to two formidable currents of thought that have recently emerged in psychology. These are the multicultural and ecopsychological viewpoints to be discussed next.

Suggested Readings

Hillman, J. (1983). *Archetypal psychology: A brief account*. Dallas, TX: Spring Publications.

Jung, C. G. (1964). *Man and his symbols*. New York: Doubleday.

Jung, C. G. (1961). *Memories, dreams, reflections* (A Jaffé, Ed.). NY: Random House.

CHAPTER 12
The Multiculturally and Ecologically Nested Personality

Margaret Mead once noted of fellow anthropologist Ruth Benedict, that Benedict considered human culture to be *personality writ large*. Similarly, anthropologist Edward T. Hall held that self-awareness and cultural awareness are inseparable. Thus, intercultural experiences can provide insights into the boundaries and contours of one's self-knowledge that would be seldom seen under normal conditions. These assertions illustrate the rationale behind cultural forms of psychology and cultural ideas pertaining to personality. Cultural psychologists hold that culture, experience, and behavior are inherently interconnected. Thus, cultural psychology is an attempt to understand how culture, experience, and behavior interact. Cultural psychology does not assume in advance that theory and research about something like personality from one culture would *necessarily* be applicable to *all* cultures. The branch of cultural psychology that focuses on comparisons and contrasts *between* cultures is called cross-cultural psychology. Cultural psychology on the whole relies on data from both within and between cultures.

Cultural psychologists David Matsumoto and Linda Juang define culture as *a unique meaning and information system, shared by a group and transmitted across generations, which allows the group to meet basic needs of survival, pursue happiness and well-being, and derive meaning from life*. As clean and thorough as this definition is, the psychological study of culture is nonetheless an extremely complicated affair due to the vast array of life factors that can influence the formation of unique and shared meaning systems. To be sure, there have been *many* attempts to identify the core constituents of culture creation throughout history. For example, below is a list of items that have been considered crucial to an understanding of culture by numerous authorities from within the social sciences.

- Ability/disability
- Age

- Artistic forms of expression
- Beliefs
- Common sense
- Education level
- Ethnicity
- Folk psychology
- Gender
- Geographic location
- Ideology
- Languages
- Marital status
- Nationality
- Norms
- Organizations
- Parental status
- Religion
- Roles
- Self-definitions
- Shared attitudes
- Social organization and status hierarchies
- Socioeconomic status
- Values

Given the size of this non-exhaustive list, it is obvious that cultures can take an amazing variety of forms. It is further obvious that cultures are nested systems. Many cultures can coexist within a given society. Further, cultures can exist within cultures, hence the rationale behind the terms *co-culture*, *subculture*, and *counterculture*.

Since it would be impossible to consider such a formidable spectrum of factors in relation to personality within the confines of a small textbook chapter, the current discussion will begin with a focus on a broad cultural dimension that implicates most of the above noted factors, especially values. This chapter will introduce *the individualism-collectivism continuum* to demonstrate how culture relates to personality. This continuum has become a prominent cultural consideration in research and theory on selfhood and personality.

For example, the individualism-collectivism continuum has played an important role in the research of Geert Hofstede in the area of organizational studies. According to Hofstede, individualism refers to the degree to which individuals in a culture are expected to be more autonomous versus more integrated into groups. In individualist cultural settings, the connections between individuals range from flexible to tenuous. Individuals are expected to look after themselves and those close to them. Collectivism, on the other hand, refers to the degree to which individuals in a culture are expected to be more connected to strong, cohesive groups, even extending outward to include distant relatives or non-relatives.

Many social scientists believe that Western cultures tend to include personalities that are more indicative of the individualist end of the individualism-collectivism continuum. Countries like the United States, Australia, the United Kingdom, the Netherlands, and New Zealand tend to rate very high in individualism. In contrast, South American and Eastern cultures tend to include personalities that are more indicative of the collectivist end of the individualism-collectivism continuum. Guatemala, Ecuador, Panama, Venezuela, and Colombia are very high on the collectivism side of the continuum. Interestingly, most research and theory pertaining to collectivism tends to focus on Asian cultures. So, for instance, places like Indonesia and Taiwan also rate very high on collectivism. However, it must be noted that collectivist personality styles are by no means exclusive to those regions of the world.

The English-speaking world is generally more accustomed to individualist values. In the United States, the term *rugged individualism* has been a commonly used phrase since President Herbert Hoover coined the term. Rugged individualism refers to the belief that individuals should be able to manage their affairs independently. According to Harry Triandis, a pioneer in cross-cultural psychology, collectivist cultures maintain a very different value system with regard to the behavior of individuals. In collectivist cultures, the self includes more *group-linked* references. In other words, individual identity is strongly linked to social context.

Along similar lines, Edward T. Hall noted cultural differences in context-relatedness in the area of intercultural communications. To express these differences, Hall introduced the terms *high-context culture* and *low-context culture*. In a high-context culture, a speaker assumes in advance that the listener already understands all sorts of things relating to the context of her communication. Speaker and listener are highly embedded within a social structure placing high value on family and community. Thus, the speaker does not assume the need to spell out many of the details of her message. There is a strong reliance on nonverbal communication. Meanings are likely to be implicit, requiring the listener to actively make sense out of a message. In a low-context culture, little is taken for granted by the speaker, so more explanation is expected in an interpersonal exchange. In a low-context culture, messages are regularly overt, explicit, simple, and clear to compensate for an implicit sense of disconnect. Thus, the message and the task at hand must have communicative priority over the relationships that contextualize the interpersonal exchange.

For some psychologists, these contrasting forms of communication are reflective of global differences in cognition or thinking style among individuals from contrasting cultures. In the area of social cognition, Richard Nisbett has noted differences in thinking style related cultural context. According to Nisbett, people who have been born and raised in individualistic cultures tend to have a more analytic style of thinking in comparison to those who have been reared in collectivist cultures. Analytical thinking is more abstract. Analytical thinkers separate things from their contexts in order to place them into discrete categories based on their distinct characteristics. In contrast, people from collectivist cultures tend to think more holistically. Holistic thinking is sensitive to the context or "field" as a whole. Holistic thinkers pay more attention to the dynamic *relationship* between things and their environments.

Differences between individualist and collectivist cultures are also evident in the area of self-other relations. Love and marriage provide relevant contrasts. In individualist cultures, it is typical that romance or feeling "in love" with another person is central to the decision to marry. People in individualistic cultures tend to experience more self-focused emotions in general when compared to people from more collectivistic backgrounds. Traditionally, there has been less emphasis on the "feeling in love" component of the marriage decision and more emphasis on things like family obligation and community expectation in collectivist cultures. In fact, the Chinese even have a word for filial piety, *xiao*. For the reader familiar with the theatre, you may recall that the tension between the desire for passion and family duty was portrayed in dramatic fashion in the play *The Fiddler on the Roof.*

Focusing on the self, Hazel Markus and Shinobu Kitayama have noted differences in *self-construals* between (individualistic) Americans and many Asian cultures. Self-construal refers to the ways in which individuals interpret, perceive, and understand themselves in relation to the world around them. Markus and Kitayama have held that contrasting self-construals account for differences in individual experience, cognition, emotion, and motivation. Self-construals in many Asian cultures are based on the assumption of a fundamental *relatedness* between individuals. The societal emphasis in these cultures is on attending to others, fitting in, and achieving harmonious interdependence. In contrast, the general norm in the United States is the development of self-construals that value independence from others and the expression of one's unique "inner" attributes.

Recently, neuroscientific studies have lent support to Markus and Kitayama's views on self-construal. Activity within the anterior rostral portion of the medial prefrontal cortex (loosely, the midsection of the frontmost portion of the cerebral cortex or MPFC, for short) is thought to reflect the neural correlate of self-knowledge. Thus, cultural neuroscientists are questioning whether the self-construals that activate this region of the brain differ depending upon where one falls along the individualist-collectivist continuum. For example, there is some evidence to support the idea that individuals from collectivist backgrounds demonstrate MPFC activation *even when presented with trait descriptors referring to someone close to them.* To this end, Joan Y. Chiao tested the possibility of cultural variations in neural activity when making trait judgments concerning self and others using functional magnetic resonance imaging (fMRI). Chiao used American and Japanese participants to examine whether collectivist personalities would show a greater response for context-dependent (i.e., relational) self-descriptions within the MPFC. Her results supported the notion that self-relevant processing within the MPFC does vary as a function of culturally related self-construal.

These findings concerning the self make sense when considering the fact that highly contextualized notions of self are pervasive among non-Western spiritual (value) traditions. For example, in the Hindu tradition emanating from India, the word *Ātman* is used to refer to the self. *Ātman* is the *true* self of an individual, which exists beyond superficial attachments and identifications with things. To achieve knowledge of the true self means realizing that *Ātman* is identical with *Brahman*. *Brahman* is the supreme, universal Spirit that is the origin and support of the universe. In Sufism, which is the mystical tradition of Islam, the self is referred to with the word *nafs*. *Nafs* is a graded phenomenon spanning various manifestations of self-development, from egocentric to self-transcendent. Examples of such manifestations are provided below.

- Inciting *nafs* (an animalistic, impulsive self)
- Inspired *nafs* (a self with the impulse to do good)
- Self-accusing *nafs* (a self with strong conscience)
- *Nafs* at peace (a non-materialistic, content self)
- Pleased *nafs* (a self that lives in the moment, accepting God's will)
- Pleasing *nafs* (a soft, tolerant self)
- Pure *nafs* (a self completely surrendered to God)

Finally, in the teachings of Zen, which is a school of Mahayana Buddhism that originated in China during the 6th century, there is no direct analogue to the self of other spiritual, cultural, and philosophical traditions. Rather, there is only a dynamic stream of consciousness that links life with life, a *bhava* or continuity of consciousness from moment to moment.

In sum, these considerations allow one to briefly characterize the opposing ends of the individualism-collectivism continuum. On one end, there are low-context, socially independent characteristics. On the other end are hi-context, socially interdependent characteristics. The characteristics that dominate each end of the spectrum are as follows.

Low-Context/
Socially Independent Characteristics
- Achieving self-consistency and identity
- Being autonomous

- Being direct
- Being unique
- Engaging in self-evaluation
- Engaging in self-expression
- Engaging in self-gratification
- Focusing on internal processes, private states, and personal needs
- Having control
- Savoring personal freedom
- Supporting one's own needs for inclusion and appreciation
- Valuing separateness
- Thinking analytically

High-Context/ Socially Interdependent Characteristics

- Being appropriate
- Being flexible
- Being subtle and indirect
- Belonging
- Feeling connected
- Fitting-in
- Fulfilling social roles
- Making external references
- Promoting others
- Promoting social harmony
- Relating
- Respecting other persons' needs for freedom or privacy
- Supporting other's needs for inclusion
- Thinking holistically

Having made these distinctions, it is critical for the reader to realize that the above noted characteristics can become part of a personality, but do not represent preestablished personality types. As Ruth Benedict once noted, no well-informed cultural scientist would assume that individuals are automatons mechanically carrying out the decrees of her culture. Moreover, the distinctions made above refer more to values than geographic locations (which, as noted above, are two different aspects of culture). Thus, for example, in

Chiao's neuropsychological studies, she found that participants' cultural *values* of individualism or collectivism modulated their neural responses within the MPFC during self-judgments, and not merely their cultural "affiliation."

Edward T. Hall made the distinction between values and geographic location long ago. For Hall, cultures display a mix of characteristics from both ends of the spectrum when it comes to individualism and collectivism. That is why I have been referring to an individualism-collectivism *continuum*. To be sure, there are both individualist and collectivist values distributed throughout the United States in differing degrees. There are various reactionary movements against the dominant rugged individualism associated with the Caucasian, Anglo-Saxon, Protestant male ethos. For example, *feminist thought* does not hold linear logic and independence in the highest esteem, but rather values community, connectedness, egalitarian process, sharing, and holism as well. The feminist ideal for the healthy personality is a balance between individual empowerment and relational competence. Feminism rejects the prevailing trend of labeling relational difficulties resulting from individualistic social norms "dependency issues." Similarly, Afrocentric thought seeks to counter the trends of Eurocentric individualism with a conscious commitment to social connectedness and spirituality rather than self-determination and individuation. Molefi Kete Asante has advocated a philosophy of *African personalism* that emphasizes the active devotion of life energy for the purpose of achieving harmony in one's personal and interpersonal life. Afrocentric thought emphasizes a communal cognitive will and the fundamental connectedness of all things, such that there is no individualized self, only a community of extended selves. Moreover, ethics and aesthetics (e.g., highly symbolic communication, musicality, and so forth) have ontological or top priority for the Afrocentric personality.

As a further demonstration of the cultural plurality found within societies, one need only consider the interpersonal and nested personality theories covered in this text, which have all been created by Westerners. By their very nature, these theories represent a countercultural force within Western psychological science, which accounts for their relative marginalization. As Calvin S. Hall and Gardner Lindzey have noted, personality theorists, especially those of the more holistic variety, have always been the rebels of psychology. In fact, the field of personality theorizing as a whole, due to its inherently relational, synoptic thrust, has traditionally failed to achieve the respect of the myopic, individualist, mainstream of psychology.

In light of the diversity inherent to cultural contexts, personality must inevitably be conceptualized in *multicultural* terms. All personalities are always multiculturally nested. In essence, multicultural personality theorizing is a sort of inversion of the factor analytic tradition of thought. The factor analytic tradition of research has sought to carve out a bare bones basic core of personality, a skeleton on which to hang the flesh of the personality, so to speak. A genuinely multicultural approach to personality moves in the opposite direction. It illuminates the intense plurality involved in personality formation due to the many factors that form the basis of those meaning and information systems used by groups to meet their various needs.

Having highlighted the distinction between values and geographic location, it must be noted that location or place can nonetheless be a powerful contextualizing force in culture creation and personality formation. To be sure, insights into the power of place have given rise to numerous "eco" orientations to psychology. The history of this kind of thinking in psychology can be traced back to Kurt Lewin's *field theory*. Lewin is considered to be a seminal figure in the emergence of social psychology. Field theory emphasized the idea that *behavior* is a direct function of the *person's* interactions with her *environment*, resulting in the heuristic formula, $B = f(P, E)$. However, Lewin focused on the "field" interpreted as the *psychological* environment of the person, the environment as interpreted and perceived as an actional life space, rather than the behavior setting in its own right. Lewin did feel that the study of the extended environment was important and noted that a psychology that would move into that area of investigation would be called a *psychological ecology*.

Readers familiar with the work of James J. Gibson and his wife Eleanor J. Gibson will note Lewin's influence on their respective "ecological" theories of perception and development. This is most easily illustrated via their work on *perceptual affordances*. From a Gibsonian point of view, perception is intimately bound to possibilities for environmental interaction. The perception of a given object or environment involves more than the apprehension of their readily obvious visual characteristics. It also involves an immediate grasp of what the object or environment "affords" in terms of possibilities for meaningful behavior.

Lewin also had an influence on Urie Bronfenbrenner, who would go on to develop *ecological systems theory*. For Bronfenbrenner, the individual human being functions as a system nested within various other interactive systems. Bronfenbrenner identified five such systems, each of which is briefly characterized below.

- *The Microsystem*: The immediate interactions that occur between the individual and her family, school, religious institution, neighborhood peers, and so forth.
- *The Mesosystem:* Relations that occur between two or more aspects of the individual's microsystem.
- *The Exosystem:* Interactions between a system in which the individual is directly involved (a microsystem) and a larger system that does not typically implicate or involve the individual.
- *The Macrosystem:* The culture in which the individual lives.
- *The Chronosystem:* The unfolding events and transitions that occur over the individual's lifespan, including the sociohistorical circumstances within which her life is unfolding.

The ecological focus on trans-individual behavior settings is still more pronounced in Roger Barker's *ecological psychology* and the *ecopsychology* of individuals like Theodore Roszak. Barker's ecological psychology focuses on the relationship between physical settings (otherwise known as *non-psychological inputs*) and behavior in general. Barker was explicit about his interest in the ecological environment beyond the psychological life space of the individual human being and insisted that the study of behavioral environments would make unique and indispensible contributions to psychology. As he noted, one can learn much about being a first baseman from a focused, concrete examination of that particular player's experiences and interactions on the ball field. However, at this close range of study, one would never learn about the rules of the game as such that govern the first baseman's overall tendencies and general repertoire of behavior. To acquire this broader form of knowledge, one would need to shift one's attention to a more global ecological viewpoint. In Barker's view, environments in the modern world change so fast and endure so much duress due to things like industrial-technological advances that the development of an ecological perspective has become imperative. This sentiment is pervasive throughout ecopsychology as well.

Ecopsychology, though very similar to ecological psychology, is a psychological application of *Gaia theory*. In ancient Greek mythology, Gaia was the goddess or personification of the Earth (i.e., "Mother Earth"). Thus, ecopsychology focuses on behavior settings with an emphasis on "nature" or "ecology" in the popularly used senses of those terms while allowing for the possibility of highly advanced interpretations of such concepts. Gaia theory holds that the organic and inorganic components of our entire planetary ecosystem are part of a single living, self-regulating system. Disturbances or perturbations in one part of the system can affect other parts of the system. Moreover, human beings are held to be an integral part of the living environment. From this point of view, human personality exists as nested within the flux and flow of the ecosystem at large. A healthy, thriving environment is correlative to healthy, thriving personalities. At the level of human nature, there is no separate, encapsulated self, only selfhood as part and parcel of the living Earth. The growing feeling of alienation from oneself, others, and the world that has been written about since at least the middle of the twentieth century stems in part from our failure to realize this inherent interconnectedness. Thus, journalist Richard Louv has coined the term *nature-deficit disorder*, while psychologist Allen D. Kanner has introduced the concept of *Mount Rushmore Syndrome*, which refers to an attitude toward nature that is grandiose, entitled, distant, dominating, manipulative, hyper-independent, and empty. An ecologically informed approach to personality proposes a new model of health that revolves around the concept of *biophilia*. Biophilia is a concept that was first introduced by the humanistic psychoanalyst Erich Fromm to designate the love of all living things.

Can things like environmental temperature, an abundance of living things (e.g., plants and animals), physical space, color, or aesthetic beauty affect personality? If so, in what ways might they affect personality? These are critical questions for an ecopsychological approach to personality. Consider the following research findings and related questions. Laboratory rats grow more rapidly in cool environments (i.e., 55° F.) than hot environments (i.e., 90° F.). When it is very hot and humid, do you find yourself moving slower or getting agitated more easily? Studies have shown that induced alterations in body temperature can have an effect on things like speed of performance on cognitive tasks, alertness, and irritability. Is your mood affected by changes of season? The *Diagnostic and Statistical Manual of Mental Disorders* includes a specifier for major depression called *seasonal affective disorder*, which is diagnosed with varying degrees of frequency in numerous countries. Alternatively, can caring, thoughtful interactions with the natural world be health-conducive? Psychologist Crystal-Helen Feral has developed an ecological connectedness model of psychotherapeutic treatment for emotionally at-risk children. Feral has found that thoughtful, involved interactions with natural settings can promote the development of things like self-esteem, happiness, perceptual skills, self-efficacy, and empathy.

What about the perception of physical space? Ethologist John B. Calhoun coined the term *behavioral sink* to describe the behavioral deterioration that results from overcrowding. Overcrowding produces a whole host of negative behaviors ranging from miscarriage, to sexual deviance, to cannibalism in laboratory rats. Along related lines, psychologist and professor of architecture Alton De Long has shown that the size dimensions of physical space have a direct effect on time perception and also of the speed of neural and cognitive processing.

Does something as simple as color affect mood or behavior? A recent study of twenty-five seasons of NHL hockey found that teams were penalized more when they wore black jerseys. Have you ever noticed that jails and schools are regularly painted in "soft" colors? A favorite in jails is what has become known as *drunk tank pink*. This is Baker-Miller Pink and it is used in hopes of calming prisoners. Businesses are careful about which colors they choose for their interior architecture and design. In fact, some mental health professionals use color exposure for therapeutic purposes, a practice referred to as chromotherapy.

Could it be that a polluted, dilapidated environment would lend itself to certain patterns of behavior as opposed to a clean, aesthetically pleasing environment? In school settings, studies have found that students in "beautiful" rooms have better attitudes and greater achievement motivation than students dwelling in "average" or "ugly" rooms.

These are all very controversial ideas, to be sure, but they do give one pause to consider the interconnection between environmental ecology and personality. At present, there is no systematic body of literature to represent a unified ecopsychological theory of personality. However, its prospects are promising, so long as ecology is not artificially isolated from its connections to culture. The potential effects of color on personality provide a clear illustration of the interconnection between the environment and culture, as colors have highly symbolic meanings that can shift and change from culture to culture. Thus, Gaian-inspired thinkers have recently begun to use terms like *transpersonal ecology* and *transpersonal ecopsychology*. Similarly, psychologists Shigehiro Oishi and Jesse Graham have recently advocated for the development of *socioecological psychology*. Finally, moral philosopher Mary Midgley has made a convincing argument that Gaian thinking leads us away from the mechanistic, reductionistic, atomistic cultural ethos of Western science and the rugged individualism so evident in the popular works of Western thinkers like Jean-Paul Sartre and Ayn Rand.

Final Remarks

What has been discussed here brings individualistic, low-context personality characteristics and collectivistic, high-context personality characteristics into full relief. More importantly, inasmuch as personality is a function of context, ecologically situated multiculturalism provides a means for appreciating the sheer diversity of personality styles that one finds among human beings. After all, human environments, in terms of both regional ecology and shared meaning systems, are remarkably diverse.

The material in this chapter not only places selfhood within a socially mediated ecosystem, it also provides a vision of optimal personality functioning based on the love of the total environment of which each of us is an integral part. Erich Fromm called this loving disposition biophilia. For Fromm, the cultural issue of socioeconomics is of prime concern for people living in the present age due to the increasing tendency among many cultures (especially American culture) to interpret all of life in terms of resources to be consumed. Fromm thus spoke of the biophilic personality as an alternative to the self envisioned as a superficial, ego-driven consumer. Thus, Fromm's work provides further insight into the dangers of rampant, unchecked individualism.

Suggested Readings

Asante, M. (1980). *Afrocentricity: Theory of social change*. Buffalo, NY: Amulefi Publishing Company.

Barker, R. (1968). *Ecological psychology: Concepts and methods for studying the environment of human behavior*. Stanford, CA: Stanford University Press.

Benedict, R. (1934). *Patterns of culture*. Boston: Houghton Mifflin.

Bronfenbrenner, U. (1981). *The ecology of human development: Experiments by nature and design*. Cambridge, MA: Harvard University Press.

Chiao, J. Y., Harada,T., Komeda, H., Li, Z., Mano, Y., Saito, D., Parrish, T. B., Sadato, N., & Iidaka, T. (2009). Neural Basis of Individualistic and Collectivistic Views of Self. *Human Brain Mapping, 30*, 2813-2820.

Davis, J. (1998). The transpersonal dimensions of ecopsychology: Nature, nonduality, and spiritual practice. *The Humanistic Psychologist, 26,* 60-100.

Feral, C. (1998). The connectedness model and optimal development: Is ecopsychology the answer to emotional well-being? *The Humanistic Psychologist, 26*, 243-274.

Fromm, E. (1955). *The sane society*. New York: Holt, Rinehart and Winston.

Fromm, E. (1956). *The art of loving*. New York: Harper & Row.

Fromm, E. (1986). *For the love of life*. NY: The Free Press.

Gibson, E. J. (1969). *Principles of perceptual learning and development*. Englewood Cliffs, NJ: Prentice Hall.

Gibson, J. J. (1986). *The ecological approach to visual perception.* Hillsdale, NJ: Lawrence Erlbaum.

Hall, E. T. (1969). *The hidden dimension.* NY: Anchor.

Hall, E. T. (1981). *Beyond culture.* NY: Anchor.

Hofstede, G. (1997). *Cultures and organizations, software of the mind: Intercultural cooperation and its importance for survival.* NY: McGraw-Hill.

Holland, R. L., Sayers, J. A., Keatinge, W. R., Davis, H. M., & Peswani, R. (1985). Effects of raised body temperature on reasoning, memory, and mood. *Journal of Applied Physiology, 59,* 1823-1827.

Kanner, A. D. (1998). Mount Rushmore Syndrome: When Narcissism Rules the Earth. *The Humanistic Psychologist, 26,* 101-122.

Lewin, K. (1935). *Dynamic theory of personality: Selected papers.* NY: McGraw-Hill.

Lewin, K. (1951). *Field theory is social science: Selected theoretical papers.* NY: Harper & Row.

Louv, R. (2008). *Last child in the woods: Saving our children from nature-deficit disorder.* NY: Algonquin.

Maslow, A. H. & Mintz, N. L. (1956). Effects of esthetic surroundings: Initial effects of three esthetic conditions upon perceiving energy and well-being in faces. *The Journal of Psychology: Interdisciplinary and Applied, 41,* 247-254.

Markus, H. R. & Kitayama, S. (1991). Culture and the self: Implications for cognition, emotion, and motivation. *Psychological Review, 98,* 224-253.

Matsumoto, D. & Juang, L. (2013). *Culture and personality.* Belont, CA: Wadsworth.

Midgley, M. (2005). *The essential Mary Midgley.* NY: Routledge.

Moore, K. (1944). The effect of controlled temperature changes on the behavior of the white rat. *Journal of Experimental Psychology, 34,* 70-79.

Nisbett, R. (2003). *The geography of thought: How Asians and Westerners think differently...and why.* NY: The Free Press.

Oishi, S. & Graham, J. (2010). Social ecology: Lost and found in psychological science. *Perspectives on Psychological Science, 5,* 356-377.

Oyserman, D., Coon, H. M., & Kemmelmeier, M. (2002). Rethinking Individualism and Collectivism: Evaluation of Theoretical Assumptions and Meta-Analyses. *Psychological Bulletin, 128*, 3-72.

Phillips, R. W. (1997). Educational facility and the academic achievement and attendance of upper elementary school students. Unpublished doctoral dissertation, University of Georgia, Athens.

Roszak, T. (1995). *Where the Wasteland Ends.* Berkeley CA: Celestial Arts.

Taylor, A. & Gousie, G. (1988). The ecology of learning environments for children. *CEFPI Journal, 26*, 23-28.

Triandis, H. C. (1995). *Individualism and collectivism.* Boulder, CO: Westview Press.

Webster, G. D., Urland, G. R., & Correll, J. (2012). Can uniform color color aggression? Quasi-experimental evidence from professional ice hockey. *Social Psychological and Personality Science, 3*, 274-281.

Chapter 13
Erich Fromm:
The Socioeconomically
Nested Personality

In order to attain a proper theoretical understanding of personality, Erich Fromm believed that one must first become cognizant of the human condition as such. One must begin one's approach to personality by starting from the fundamental predicament that *all* human beings find themselves in. In other words, Fromm insisted upon grounding his ideas about personality in an *anthropologico-philosophical concept of human existence.*

For Fromm, human beings have evolved beyond the more decisive, more thoroughgoing union within nature that one finds among the rest of the animal kingdom. Human beings are one step removed from their animal nature and, as a result, they are unable to wholly rely on innate biological mechanisms like instincts to guide the development of their personalities. Even more so than Freud, Fromm was skeptical of the notion of human "instincts." The reason for this is that the criteria for something to qualify as a genuine instinct are formidable. Instincts are inborn or innate, triggered more or less automatically, species-wide, rather inflexible across members of a species, and relatively complex in that they involve many actions (i.e., they are not mere reflexes, but fixed action patterns). For a species as diverse as ours, that is a tall order to fill. Fromm is not opposed to the idea that human beings have drives or rely on a genetic and biological endowment. Rather, he points out that human beings and human personality formation are far more reliant on learning, reason, imagination, decision-making, and self-reflective knowledge than any other creature on the planet.

This situation has evolved for a productive reason. Human beings are more efficient and effective at adapting to diverse environments than other animal species. The human population keeps growing while something on the order of one hundred and fifty to two hundred species of plant, insect, bird, and mammal become extinct every day (about one thousand times the "natural" rate of extinction). Thus, the flexibility inherent to human adaptability clearly has drawbacks as well.

Fromm points out that self-reflective knowledge makes it possible for human beings to agonize over certain mysteries, riddles, or paradoxes that become apparent upon the development of conscious awareness. Fromm referred to these paradoxes as *existential dichotomies* because they refer to fundamental contradictions inherent to human existence. In Fromm's view, all human beings are alike in the sense that they share the same basic human predicament and same existential dichotomies, but they are each unique in their specific ways of dealing with these shared conditions, and that is the foundation for his approach to personality.

Fromm's first existential dichotomy results from the fact that self-reflective, conscious awareness bequeaths human beings with a heightened appreciation for life. However, this very appreciation makes the sting of death all the more painful. A human being can savor her life in a deep and meaningful way, but all the while she knows that the life she so relishes must be taken from her.

The second existential dichotomy relates to the fact that human beings must orchestrate their lives and cooperatively create their personalities by making decisions. This brings with it a desire to fulfill one's potentials, to imagine and envision an ideal toward which one's would work over the course of the lifespan. As Alfred Adler had shown, human development is rooted in the desire to feel ever more complete and fulfilled. However, human beings are both fallible and limited in terms of their abilities and resources. In effect, reflective awareness brings with it the exhilarating perception of possibilities for realizing skills, talents, hopes, dreams, and aspirations, but these are never fully realizable. Human existence always bears the mark of a fundamental incompleteness. There will always be stones unturned, potentials untapped, risks not taken. There will always be more to see, more to learn, more to do. Fulfillment must always be provisional and therefore, at least somewhat disappointing.

The third and final existential dichotomy arises from the realization that we are all part of a cosmic ecology and an ancestry. Human beings come to realize that they live among others and among nature. During peak experiences, this feeling of being connected to the whole of the living universe is highly pronounced.

Yet, at the same time, all humans feel the undeniable reality of our fundamental aloneness from the outset of human development (e.g., think of Erikson's basic anxiety). Individuality cannot simply be abandoned, hard as one might try. Reflective awareness and decision making give human beings the ability to become independent, which is often experienced as exhilarating, but it is equally true that human beings detest isolation and loneliness.

According to Fromm, the disharmony inherent to the human condition (i.e., the difficulties created by the lack of life-governing instincts) generates a need for human beings to creatively restore unity and equilibrium between themselves and nature. To this end, human beings develop a striving for personality integration in the form of "unified character." *Character orientations* provide an organized means for finding tentative "solutions" to existential dichotomies and allow people to live a fulfilled life in spite of the fact that existential dichotomies cannot be simply eradicated. For Fromm, answers to the problems of existence will inevitably be sought in strategic attempts to satisfy five human needs. These are the need for *relatedness*, the need for *transcendence*, the need for *rootedness*, the need for an *identity*, and the need for a *frame of orientation*. Like the striving for character, Fromm believed that these needs also arise from the basic human situation of being dislodged from nature.

In Fromm's view, the patterned ways that human beings go about searching for answers to the problems of existence (i.e., their character orientations) are a direct function of sociocultural and economic context. In what follows, I will discuss the five human needs identified by Fromm and how they address existential dichotomies. I will then outline Fromm's thoughts on the socioeconomic context of contemporary character development. I will conclude with an overview of several character orientations mentioned in Fromm's works.

Fromm considered the need for relatedness and rootedness to be particularly effective at managing the pain of separation and aloneness. Relatedness is the desire for union with the world and other people. In unhealthy people, this desire manifests itself in the form of either submission to others or the impulse to have power over the world and other people. Submissives and power mongers seek a *symbiotic relationship* with the world around them and can be said to be in denial concerning the impossibility of erasing the existential dichotomy implicated in human individuality. Furthermore, they are inherently *narcissistic* in their inability to care for others as distinct individuals. This is not so for healthy people. The healthy person seeks relatedness through love, which does not seek complete merger, but authentic *relation*-ship. Love comes is several forms, including brotherly love, motherly love, erotic love, *genuine* self-love (which is the opposite of selfishness), and the love of God.

Rootedness is the desire to feel connected and at home in the world. Unhealthy individuals shy away from the challenges inherent to laying down roots somewhere and making a home. Instead, they remain *fixated*, by which Fromm means an incestuous, passive reluctance to move beyond the protective home environment provided by one's mother. In healthy circumstances, people play an active role in creating warm, welcoming environments like a home.

Fromm considered transcendence and identity to be particularly efficacious at handling the problem of human incompleteness. Transcendence is the desire to rise above a passive, accidental existence into the realm of productive freedom and purpose. It is the urge to be a creator rather than just a creature. In the unhealthy person, the inherent striving to create is somehow or other thwarted. When this happens, the urge to create is transmuted into the urge to *destroy*. Fromm is clear that the striving toward death and destruction and the striving toward life and creation are not total and complete opposites, since both creation and destruction are forms of active involvement in the world. In both instances, the individual can feel gratified that she took good advantage of the possibility of doing something that was her own, even if the project was not completed.

Identity refers to the capacity to become aware of oneself as a unique individual. A person with an identity has a sense of personal responsibility for her own values, beliefs, emotions, actions, and so forth. In spite of the inability to "complete" oneself, there is a sense of gratification associated with the active exploration of life's many opportunities and the feeling of "owning" one's life. Unhealthy people do not have the resilience and perseverance to do the soul searching needed for identity formation. Instead, they opt to live life via a *herd-like conformity and a blind obedience to authority*.

Finally, a frame of orientation provides an additional tool for dealing with the problem of incompleteness, as well as a means to manage the sting of death. To have developed a frame of orientation means that one has sketched out a mental schematic for interpreting and making sense out of life. The world, with all of its complexities, ambiguities, and dichotomies, cries out for meaning and sense. Fromm held that human beings can use reason and imagination to put one's incompleteness in perspective and thereby make the problems of life feel that much less overwhelming and unmanageable. A frame of orientation is also a global philosophy of life and the relationship of life to death. Healthy people seek out reason and apply it in an embodied, impassioned, imaginative way to make sense out of their lives and eventual deaths. Unhealthy people avoid reason and consciously or unconsciously maintain *irrational* views of human life on earth.

All in all, there is no guarantee that a person will find adequate answers to the problems of human existence. For Fromm, much depends on one's sociocultural predicament. In particular, Fromm was keenly aware of the difficulties inherent to healthy personality formation in a society where the individual is faced with adversity that is socioeconomic in origin. The United States of America provides a particularly clear example of the adversity that Fromm had in mind.

Americans are put in a rather precarious situation by virtue of the fact that we live amid two very powerful, yet incongruous social forces. On the one hand, American's enjoy unprecedented freedom and embrace this freedom as a top value. America is, after all, "the home of the free." At the same time, marketers are free to bombard us with a constant stream of messages telling us who we *ought* to be. Americans live amid both high levels of political freedom and a commodity market capable of powerfully influencing not only our economic activity, but our entire manner of social relatedness. Politically speaking, we enjoy much freedom *from* rules, regulations, dictates, and so forth, but this is just one aspect of freedom, and it is not enough to facilitate fulfillment and healthy personality formation. Freedom must be used productively in the interest of love, creativity, establishing roots, identity formation, and the development of a frame of orientation in order that a robust sense of self may be realized. However, rather than being part of a concerted effort to put our freedom to positive use, Americans live under the constant pressure to have and consume the "right" kinds of products. Corporations have increasingly worked to commandeer our freedom *to be* and replaced it with a mere freedom to have and expend. As a result, many people feel uneasy in the face of their freedom.

According to Fromm, modern capitalism seeks masses of cooperative people who will habitually consume according to standardized tastes that can be easily influenced and anticipated. It needs people who only *feel* free, but who are in reality quite ready to follow anyone who might appear to have a remedy for the anxiety associated with freedom without productive purpose. As life becomes less about cooperative being and more about competitive having, freedom comes to feel more and more like a burden (though few would readily admit of this, especially in a political climate like the United States). The result is that human beings in highly consumeristic social climates have come to be increasingly alienated from themselves, others, and nature. Self-realization remains elusive. The rock band The Rolling Stones captured the emotional conflict of this predicament in their song *(I Can't Get No) Satisfaction* with the lyrics, "When I'm watchin' my TV and a man comes on to tell me how white my shirts can be, well he can't be a man 'cause he doesn't smoke the same cigarettes as me."

Before moving forward, it should be noted that Fromm was careful to single out *modern* capitalism, which has become highly corporatized and consumeristic, rather than *all* capitalism for his sociocultural critiques. Fromm was also willing to admit of the positive attributes of cultural individualism inasmuch as individualism can promote the uniqueness and dignity of the individual. Fromm did, however, oppose the superficial, empty, rugged individualism that modern capitalism produces. He believed that modern (i.e., corporatized, consumeristic) capitalism lends itself to the development of various non-productive character orientations.

As was noted earlier, human beings develop organized strategies in an attempt to find answers to the problems of human existence, which Fromm referred to as character orientations. Some attempts to develop unified character are productive and healthy, while others are non-productive. Fromm identified several non-productive character orientations that he believed were a reflection of the socioeconomic cultural conditions described above. For example, those who display *receptive character* feel that all that is good comes from outside themselves. Accordingly, their primary concern is with receiving things (e.g., love, gifts, even personal style and ideas). Those who display *exploitive character* are similar to receptive individuals, but they do not expect to be given things, so they aggressively take what they want from others. People with *hoarding character* orientations seek to save what they have gained and not let anything go. They are the misers of the world, and their preoccupation is with keeping things inside the walls of their protective psychological stronghold. Individuals who display a *marketing character* orientation are a direct reflection of modern commerce. These people see themselves as commodities on the market. Their personal value is felt to be dependent on their ability to sell themselves.

Receptive, exploitive, hoarding, and marketing character orientations are more or less garden variety attempts to achieve personal integration. However, Fromm also identified three unification strategies that he considered *regressive* or pathological character orientations. The first of these is called *necrophilia*, by which Fromm meant the love of death and destruction in all of its forms. The second regressive orientation is called *narcissism*, meaning an intense attachment to oneself or one's groups that distorts rational judgment. The third regressive orientation is called *incestuous symbiosis*, which is a condition wherein a person remains so attached to her mother that self-development is more or less abandoned.

In contrast to these character orientations, Fromm described what he called a *productive character* orientation. The productive character orientation refers to the healthy personality. This orientation is associated with the rational and imaginative employment of *positive freedom*. That is, people who display the productive orientation use their freedom to create, to innovate, and to be generative, but in a deeply meaningful, aesthetically, and ethically cultural sense foreign to the corporate-consumer mindset. Fromm held that human beings are not merely rational and social, they are also creative and productive. For him, productiveness is the quintessential realization of human potential. Productiveness is gauged by a person's loving dedication to the mutual flourishing of self, others, and the whole of the natural world. Only through this *biophilic* style is a human being capable of experiencing deep, robust personality integration.

Final Remarks

Erich Fromm's personality theory reminds us that neither the human condition nor the socioeconomic context of human affairs can be ignored in personality theorizing. Fromm's theory provides novel insights into the nature of both healthy and the unhealthy personalities. His socially informed critiques outline several compelling ways in which consumeristic culture can impede optimal personality functioning (i.e., his non-productive and pathological character orientations). Indeed, the current popularity of American reality programs that require individuals to "sell" themselves, as well as those that focus on human hoarding, gives one a sense that Fromm was ahead of his time.

Fromm's focus on both a universal human condition and the socioeconomic context of personality formation constitutes a refutation of cultural relativism in its pure form. Fromm is clear that cultures can be healthy or sick depending on their ability to help human beings find answers to the fundamental problems of human existence. For Fromm, the relative health or sickness of a culture can affect the lives of the individuals who live in that culture. Contemporary corporatized cultures take *Homo sapiens* and turn them into *Homo consumens,* says Fromm. On a mass scale, the members of modern capitalism suffer from what has recently been dubbed *affluenza.* Though it might be tempting to interpret Fromm as saying that the contemporary preoccupation with having and consuming is the result of selfishness, Fromm would have found such an interpretation superficial. He believed that people lack genuine self-love and have been emptied of all substance to make way for an overriding consumer impulse. Fromm saw that human beings on a mass scale have become alienated from the depth, meaning, and harmony of a biophilic lifestyle by the tantalizing, stimulating lures of habitual consumption.

Still, Fromm was not devoid of hope. Fromm maintained that social change was not only needed, but possible by way of pedagogy and educational reform. For Fromm, to educate is to bring out potentials for self-realization and promote authenticity. More and more, however, educational systems appear to be making automatons, functional cogs in the big machinery of corporate culture. Instead, it should be helping students respond to the world with their senses in a meaningful, skilled, productive, active, and shared way. Fromm calls this outcome of education *collective art*, since our language currently has no word for such a state of being. Here, Fromm is following Alfred Adler who once noted that in order to attain a proper understanding of a child's lifestyle, one must develop an artistic manner of thinking and perceiving.

Fromm felt that students should learn to become skilled with their hands, as Maria Montessori once noted, so that there is a balance of both mind and body in the learning process. It is important to feel the value of creative production with one's own hands, which is a phenomenological insight relating to the fact that touch provides the most meaningful and intimate form of contact with the world. Good pedagogy, Fromm held, was vital to the development of the sane society. Fromm believed that there are those among us who can see through the trappings consumer culture and can help others live productively. Similar to Alfred Adler before him, Fromm believed that what matters most is how each person interprets and appropriates the raw materials of self-development and personality formation provided by her environmental context.

Suggested Readings

de Graaf, J., Wann, D., & Naylor, T. H. (2005). *Affluenza: The all-consuming epidemic*. San Francisco, CA: Berrett-Koehler Publishers.

DeRobertis, E. M. (2008). *Humanizing child developmental theory: A holistic approach*. New York: iUniverse.

DeRobertis, E. M. (2012). *The whole child: Selected papers on existential-humanistic child psychology*. Charleston, SC: CreateSpace Publishing.

Fromm, E. (1947). *Man for himself: An inquiry into the psychology of ethics*. New York: Holt, Rinehart and Winston.

Fromm, E. (1955). *The sane society*. New York: Holt, Rinehart and Winston.

Fromm, E. (1956). *The art of loving*. New York: Harper & Row.

Fromm, E. (1986). *For the love of life*. NY: The Free Press.

Chapter 14
Rollo May: The Narratively Nested, Destining Personality

Rollo May belongs to the same meta-theoretical or philosophical tradition of thought as Viktor Frankl. Both are existential psychologists who have had occasion to engage in phenomenological description as well. To review, existentialism is an intellectual movement that stresses the fact that human beings are not solely or even primarily thinkers. Rather, humans are first and foremost caring, choosing, and acting beings. This does not mean that humans are not thinkers, of course. Quite the contrary, thought is very important to existentialists since thought is vital to individual accountability and responsibility. Perhaps one could say that rather than claiming, "I think, therefore I am," existentialists claim, "I *am*, therefore I think." To existential thinkers, like Martin Heidegger, for example, a human being is not a detached observer of the world, but rather a feeling, desiring *being-in-the-world-with-others-alongside-things*. The hyphens are meant to denote the fact that self, others, and nature together form an intimately intertwined dynamic system. There is no separation of mind from body or person from world. Human beings always find themselves *ahead* of themselves, always *already caught-up* in worldly affairs as a natural state of their being.

For groundbreaking existential philosophers like Kierkegaard and Heidegger, questions of authentic selfhood and personal identity were of utmost importance. Existential thought traditionally emphasizes the importance of taking ownership and responsibility for one's life, committing oneself to courses of action that demonstrate a belief in the personal meaning of one's behavior, and thoughtfully examining the impact of one's actions on oneself, others, and the world. Human beings have the power to redefine themselves and expand their scope of awareness through devoted, conscientious action. This process leads to the development of traits like conscience, integrity, and resoluteness.

Rollo May takes this template and extends it by saying that this process of personal transformation allows human beings to find and fulfill a *destiny*. Before moving on, however, it is important to note that destiny is not fate. Existentialists do not believe in fate. Life is viewed as a project to be carried out. The final form of the lifespan is not given in advance of individual involvement. The task of every human being is to answer the question, "What is the meaning of the life that I have been given?" To address this question is to address the issue of destiny. Destiny is the true purpose of one's life, one's personal mission or calling. It involves an inspired dedication or commitment that would tend to creatively bring about the growth and fulfillment of oneself, others, and the world at large (i.e., the entire structure of being-in-the-world-with-others-alongside-things). Thus, a real destiny cannot be selfish in any of the pejorative senses of that word.

To live in accord with one's destiny is a quintessential expression of healthy personality formation in May's works. For May, there are a number of foundational elements that make the process of finding and fulfilling one's destiny possible. These include *intentionality*, *care*, *love*, *will*, and *myth*. May does not use the word intentionality the way that Albert Bandura and others in psychology typically use the term. Intentionality does not mean merely that human beings sometimes do things "on purpose," as it were. May's concept originates in the works of Edmund Husserl, the father of phenomenology. For May, the word intentionality denotes the fact that the human mind is always connected to the world in a meaningful, interactive manner. The fact that human beings are intentional, in this sense, means that they never live within the confines of their own skulls with nothing but a mass of worldless, anonymous "sense data." Intentionality is what makes it possible for human beings to truly live *in and with* a coherent world of things and other people. Accordingly, phenomenological intentionality is the ultimate basis upon which "doing something on purpose" would ever come to pass.

In addition to being intentional, May noted that human beings display the characteristic of care. Here, May drew inspiration from Martin Heidegger. Again, care, in this context, means something more fundamental than the commonsense and popular psychological notions of gentleness and devotion. By care, May meant to highlight a fundamental characteristic of human intentionality, which is its mooded, emotionally invested nature. As May conceptualized it, care is a state in which things matter (and there are many ways in which they can matter). Human beings are not involved in worldly affairs primarily in the form of an intellectualized, rationalized detachment. Human beings are not first and foremost fledgling scientists, as some developmental psychologists might have it. It is our nature to be both intellectually *and affectively caught up* in-the-world-with-others-alongside-things. Meaningful involvement in the world, in other words, means something more than just data transfer and information processing. Human beings are engaged in projects and relationships that implicate their very being, their self-development as such. Thus, referencing Heidegger, May once noted that when fully conceived, care implicates selfhood.

Optimally, love and will are added to intentionality and care. May defines love in general as a delight that one experiences in the presence of another person while affirming her inherent value. However, May believed that there are four different (though not mutually exclusive) manifestations of love in the world of human affairs. First, there is *philia*, friendship, or brotherly love. Second, there is sex, lust, or *libido*. Third, there is *eros*, which is the drive to love, create, or procreate with others. Eros refers to cooperative involvement aimed at achieving increasingly creative forms of relational being. Fourth and finally, there is *agape*, which is love that is primarily devoted to the welfare of the other, the prototype of which is the love of God for humanity.

According to Rollo May, love breeds and feeds acts of *will*. The love of something or someone is unparalleled in its ability to mobilize potentials for organized, deliberate action. Thus, May defined will as the capacity to organize one's personal resources so that movement toward a certain goal may take place. Willing is care and love in action and the embodied actualization of intentionality. As May phrased it, willing is caring "made free." Thus, will is sometimes referred to as freewill and goodwill.

The last main element of healthy personality formation is myth. Myth, in Rollo May's works does not mean a falsehood, as it does in everyday discourse. May's usage is more true to the original meaning of myth as *mythos*, which is also used in other disciplines like anthropology and sociology. For May, myths are the linguistic housing of a culture's beliefs, values, attitudes, and so forth. Myths are the stories that dispatch time honored truths to the members of a culture across space and time. Healthy personality formation requires structure, direction, and a framework of meanings and values to operate within. Human beings, as Fromm had also noted, need inspiration, hope, guidance and life perspective. In short, the achievement of optimal personality functioning requires access to templates or schematic prototypes for finding and fulfilling a destiny. The idea is, shared stories found personal life narratives. In this sense, May's concept of destiny is an advanced version of Alfred Adler's final fiction, which May readily admitted in his book on myth.

Myths are unifiers at both the social and personal level. Myths inspire the courageous search for personal identity and destiny, even in the face of hardship (e.g., think of David and Goliath or the trials and tribulations of your favorite superhero for that matter). To call a cultural myth a falsehood or say it is "just" a story is to miss its core meaning entirely. Myths house explicit and implicit belief systems that provide perspective and give meaning to social and personal problems. Myths are like the support beams of a house. They are the grand narratives that unite groups and societies and, under ideal conditions, direct their actions toward growth oriented aims. To have words and sense-making narratives is to be deeply empowered. Words and narratives help human beings achieve stability, balance, purpose, and fulfillment in a complex, confusing, and often challenging world.

Unfortunately, in many contemporary, industrialized cultures, positivistic and spiritual narratives have come to be pit against one another, as if one kind of *mythos* is necessarily right and the other simply false. More generally, positivistic science is considered fact, while all other narratives (e.g., personal, familial, communal, societal, or spiritual) are considered "mere" stories. The problem with this situation is that positivism, due to its rationalist nature, seeks "only the facts" (or, better, its version of "the facts"). The ideal of positivistic science is to be *value-free*. Thus, positivism offers a *mythos* that provides much intelligence, but very little wisdom, much knowledge, but little to comfort the striving, struggling, suffering soul.

In addition to its claim of value neutrality (which, incidentally, is far from certain), positivistic science interprets human beings as so much biological machinery. A human being is a bio-machine, no different from any other *thing* in the natural world in any substantial way. If something like personal subjectivity is granted in some small measure, that subjectivity is viewed as locked within the cranium of the individual in question. This has come to be compounded by the fact that human beings are increasingly looked upon as human resources or human capital in the industrial and post-industrial ages. Moreover, our growing reliance on and fascination with technology means human beings are becoming incidental to societies sources of mass production if not altogether obsolete. All of these factors have lead to the gradual erosion of the edifice of healthy personality formation described by May. Intentionality appears to yield pointlessness, absurdity, and insignificance. Care is being replaced by isolation, loneliness, boredom, and apathy. Love is being replaced by lust and narcissism. Will is being replaced by irresponsibility, helplessness, indecisiveness, and aggression. Myth is being replaced by resignation and a burgeoning interest in cults and cult membership. Finally, destiny is being replaced by confusion and anonymity. These cultural changes prompted Rollo May to refer to contemporary times as an *age of melancholy*.

May, following philosopher Paul Tillich, believed this melancholy to be rooted in *the spiritual anxiety of emptiness and meaninglessness*. May further felt that this anxiety has become so powerfully overwhelming that it is giving rise to increasing levels of neurotic anxiety. Rollo May made a distinction between *normal anxiety*, which he believed to be associated with the typical challenges of living, and *neurotic anxiety*. Normal anxiety is a sign of eustress and the fact that one has a substantive, meaningful life full of valued projects and relationships. In an imperfect world, the failure of any of one's projects and relationships is always a possibility, but one perseveres nonetheless out of a dedication to that which is valued. Normal anxiety is productive in that it sharpens the senses and opens one up to the world-with-others-alongside-things. However, neurotic anxiety is destructive, as it is akin to a form of panic wherein one is closed off to the world. In a state of neurotic anxiety, insight becomes elusive. If left unresolved, feelings of isolation, depersonalization, and apathy set in.

As a result of the pain associated with it, May noted that people seek shelter from neurotic anxiety through self-deception (e.g., defense mechanisms) and by relying on distractions that temporarily cover over the emptiness and meaninglessness in which neurotic anxiety is rooted. Things like promiscuous sex, drugs, television, food, alcohol, the Internet, and so forth provide temporary relief from the crushing realization of one's global psycho-spiritual impoverishment. Unfortunately, however, when a person avoids making choices that would promote the discovery of a destiny and the development of an authentic identity, one only feels increasingly impoverished and existentially guilty. Existential guilt is a guilt that implicates one's entire choice of lifestyle. It is rooted in the unavoidable knowledge that life is time limited, but despite the fact that every moment counts, one is squandering these moments. Thus, what is called for is a cessation of avoidance, a refusal to succumb to the tantalizing lures of a culture that prefers automatons to human beings. What is called for is a renewed commitment to the task of creating a life narrative that promotes the emergence of *authentic selfhood*, lovingly in-the-world-with-others-alongside-things. For Rollo May, this kind of commitment is what distinguishes the healthy personality from the unhappy, unfulfilled personalities of our times.

Final Remarks

Rollo May outlined a holistic, systemic foundation for personality theorizing. He did through his particular psychological interpretation and application of Martin Heidegger's notion of being-in-the-world-alongside-things. Being primarily a psychologist rather than a philosopher, May's application of existential thought allows one to address issues pertaining to the relative health of human beings. Healthy personality formation rests on a dynamic, world-relating foundation of intentionality, care, love, will, myth, and destiny.

For May, one cannot properly understand personality formation without accounting for the worldly context within which the individual lives. A crucial feature of this context is the narrative structures or stories that human beings live by. May did not consider contemporary industrialized and post-industrialized cultures to be conducive to health, and noted that they have become want of reliable narratives to support human becoming. As a consequence, the present age is increasingly giving rise to phenomena like pointlessness, absurdity, insignificance, personal isolation, loneliness, boredom, apathy, lust, narcissism, irresponsibility, helplessness, indecisiveness, aggression, confusion, resignation, blind obedience, anonymity, emptiness, meaninglessness, depression, and neurotic anxiety. Along with Fromm, May highlighted the pressing need for social reform on a large, culture-wide scale. Like Fromm, May emphasized the need for human beings to resist socializing forces that are not only unhealthy, but homogenize human beings, strip them of their potential for authenticity, and make them unreflective herd animals or bio-mechanisms. Stated differently, Fromm and May both underscored the importance of what Abraham Maslow called *resistance to enculturation.*

Tellingly, both Erich Fromm and Rollo May dedicated places in their respective theories to the study of love in particular. Both theorists felt that any discussion of personality would be incomplete without addressing the varieties of love and noting the importance of love for personality formation. All in all, it seems that both theorists perceived there to be an inherent connectivity between the healthy personality, the authentic personality, and the loving personality. As May once observed, narcissism and unbridled self-interest actually *destroy* individuality, as contradictory as that might seem. Looking back, I think the reader will agree that this idea has been slowly but surely emerging since at least the sixth chapter.

Suggested Readings

Heidegger, M. (1962). *Being and time.* New York: Harper Collins.

May, R. (1953). *Man's search for himself.* NY: W. W. Norton.

May, R. (1969). *Love and will.* NY: W. W. Norton.

May, R. (1979). *Psychology and the human dilemma.* NY: W. W. Norton.

May, R. (1991). *The cry for myth.* NY: W. W. Norton.

May, R., Angel, E., and Ellenberger H. (1958). *Existence: A new dimension in psychiatry and psychology.* New York: Basic Books.

Tillich, P. (1980). *The courage to be.* New Haven: Yale University Press.

Epilogue

This small textbook provided the reader with a sampling of theories that expose significant aspects of human personality. I hope to have shown that each theory has made valuable contributions to the development of a holistic, synoptic understanding of personality. The text began by noting the fact that genetic endowment provides foundational structure and forward moving (adaptive) directionality to personality formation. However, neither ontogeny nor phylogeny is destiny. Human begins are born with a *predisposition* to develop certain kinds of traits over others, but human personality is mutable, plastic, and subject to repeated transformations over the course of the lifespan.

Behavioral theories proved to be valuable to personality theorizing because the behaviorists shed light on a major source of this plasticity. The behaviorists demonstrated that repeated interactions with specific environments create conditioned responses. They further noted the impressive power of reinforcement in molding and shaping personality. By giving the power of rewarding stimulation a central place in their thinking, the behaviorists shared some significant theoretical common ground with Sigmund Freud. At the same time, Freud observed that the striving for pleasure has to be counterbalanced by ego and superego development if an individual is to coexist with others. Freud's articulation of these counterbalancing forces exposed the depth of meaning involved in personality formation, especially in its frustrated, conflicted, and pathological aspects.

With the introduction of cognitive social learning perspectives, personality was viewed in a more self-regulating, agentic light. This was due to the cognitive social learning theorists' perceptions of the power of the human intellect in shaping personality. Cognitive social learning approaches noted how the active, interpretive intellect is informed by the past to deal with the contingencies of the here-and-now, and to plan for a possible future. Moreover, individual cognitive processes were observed to have ongoing reciprocal relations to the cognitive processes of others and the world at large.

Erik Erikson's psychosocial ego theory contributed an impressive breadth of socially derived emotionality to the agency inherent to human personality. Whereas Freud provided an undercurrent of tumultuous emotionality to personality theorizing, Erikson provided a means to journey in an opposing direction. Erikson showed how functional interpersonal relationships can give rise to various strengths or virtues indicative of the truly personal in personality.

The theories of William Stern and Gordon Allport introduced the reader to concepts such as person and proprium (i.e., selfhood). Stern and Allport each, in their own ways, decisively exposed the core of human personality by highlighting the warmth, the sense of ownership, and the dynamic unity of the individual. Stern outlined the various hierarchically interrelated aspects of the person, while Allport detailed the diverse aspects of both the proprium and the personality as a whole. In spite of this plurality, personality was shown to be a goal-directed *unitas multiplex*.

Alfred Adler brought the warmth and goal-directed unity of human personality more squarely within the realm of interpersonal relations. In order to do so, Adler emphasized the fact that personality formation is the result of cooperative creative effort. Personality formation is, in great measure, a reflection of one's social world. In particular, Adler emphasized the fact that healthy personality development is best facilitated in an environment conducive to social interest. The creative self is only really nurtured when capable of developing, maintaining, and fostering community feeling.

Karen Horney and Carl Rogers extended this line of thought by detailing the maternal and familial conditions most conducive to the development of selfhood. In addition, Horney and Rogers raised the significant issue of the relative genuineness of the personality. Rogers and Horney both observed that self-development must proceed unimpeded by conditions of worth that would compromise the personal insight, wholeheartedness, and psycho-emotional integrity of the individual.

With the theories of Abraham Maslow and Viktor Frankl, the transcendent self came into focus. For Maslow, self-transcendence was more or less connected to exceptional states of consciousness. For Frankl, the concept of self-transcendence had meaning for day-to-day living as well. In spite of their differences, both Maslow and Frankl highlighted the inherently meaningful, value-laden interpenetration of person and world. They each dedicated focused attention to the profound connectivity of human personality with the whole of the universe.

Carl Jung's personality theory marked the beginning of a series of discussions having a dedicated focus on the contextual forces involved in personality formation. In Jung's work, one finds the personality nested within an ancestry. The components of this ancestry were found to be embedded within human culture. Jung saw the personality as structured in accord with the transcendent function of the archetypal self.

Jung's emphasis on culture then lead to an acknowledgment of the inherently multicultural nature of all human personalities. As an illustration of the power of culture, the concepts of individualism and collectivism were reviewed. In addition, the importance of geographic location by way of natural ecology was discussed. In this regard, the need for a systematic, unified body of ecopsychological literature on personality was noted. Erich Fromm's notion of the biophilic personality was introduced as a guiding concept for the ecologically nested personality.

Erich Fromm contributed to the contextualization of personality by illuminating the ways in which the socioeconomic environment can influence an individual. Fromm saw that the uniquely human striving to attain a unified character orientation is sensitive to the values embedded within one's sociopolitical and economic milieu. Fromm warned that in today's day and age, rampant consumerism has made it more difficult than ever to achieve biophilia. Fromm's theory stands as a testament to the contemporary relevance of individual discernment when it comes to enculturation. Specifically, Fromm stressed the need to think, feel, and act in ways that are at variance with the forces of mass culture. Personality formation thus involves the emergence of an authentic self, standing in loving defiance of the anonymity fostered by corporatized culture.

Rollo May's theory provided a fitting means for understanding the integration of the personality at its highest levels of analysis. May pointed out that the striving to find and fulfill a destiny is a vitalizing, integrative force like no other. May shared Fromm's sentiments concerning the need for authentic, biophilic selfhood, noting that the anonymity that appears to be engulfing humanity is further rooted in depersonalizing positivistic and technological life narratives. As existential psychologist Edward L. Murray once noted, healthy personality formation is dependent upon robust myths, life narratives rich in literal, symbolic, and metaphorical meaning that can act as a guide for navigating life's broad array of challenges.

Suggested Readings

Murray, E. L. (1986). *Imaginative thinking and human existence.* Pittsburgh, PA: Duquesne University Press.

Murray, E. L. (1987). *Imagination and phenomenological psychology.* Pittsburgh: Duquesne University Press.

Murray, E. L. (2001). *The quest for personality integration: Reimaginizing our lives.* Pittsburgh: Simon Silverman Phenomenology Center.

About the Author

Eugene M. DeRobertis holds a B.A. in philosophy from St. Peter's College and a Ph.D. in psychology from Duquesne University. He has been a college professor since 1996. Prior to committing himself to teaching full-time, Dr. DeRobertis worked as a developmentally oriented psychotherapist and addictions counselor. His most recent academic authorship focuses on applying existential-phenomenological humanism to the study of child development.

Dr. DeRobertis was born in Hoboken, New Jersey on September 2, 1970. He spent his formative years learning working class values in suburban New Jersey. As a youngster, Dr. DeRobertis played intramural sports, learned to play the guitar, and took an interest in automobiles. Upon completing high school he intended to follow in his father's footsteps by working on the railroad. However, at the urging of his mother, Dr. DeRobertis enrolled at St. Peter's College as a marketing management major.

Dissatisfied with the prospect of a career in business, he decided to pursue his passion for philosophy. In 1992, Dr. DeRobertis graduated St. Peter's College and received the school's Rankin Medal for achieving the highest grade point average in philosophy of any student in his graduating class. While studying at St. Peter's, Dr. DeRobertis developed a strong interest in existential-phenomenology. As a result, he applied to Duquesne University and began studying existential-phenomenological psychology there in September of 1992. While completing his doctorate, Dr. DeRobertis worked as a psychotherapist and an adjunct psychology professor. In addition, he completed his first text, an introduction to phenomenological psychology, in 1996.

Since receiving his Ph.D., Dr. DeRobertis has written on a host of topics, including the impact of contemporary information technology on interpersonal relations, childhood psychological maltreatment, theoretical and philosophical psychology, phenomenology, and existential-humanistic child developmental theory. He currently works for Brookdale College and Rutgers University.

Other academic titles by Eugene M. DeRobertis

- *Humanizing Child Developmental Theory: A Holistic Approach.* NY: iUniverse, 2008. ISBN-13: 978-0595449248

- *The Whole Child: Selected Readings in Existential-Humanistic Child Psychology.* Charleston, SC: CreateSpace, 2012. ISBN-13: 978-1477635759

- *Existential-Phenomenological Psychology: A Brief Introduction.* Charleston, SC: CreateSpace, 2012. ISBN-13: 978-1478173557

Other books by Eugene M. DeRobertis

- *The Loser Magnet Handbook: A Quick Guide to Understanding the Romantically Challenged.* NY: iUniverse, 2008. ISBN-13: 978-0595487127 (Also available in kindle edition.)

Poetry titles by Arlene M. DeRobertis

- *A Star Beyond The Thistle Moon: Images of Adversity and Hope.* (2012) ISBN-13: 978-1475142433

- *Triumph of the Soul: Images of Anguish, Awe, and Inspiration.* (2012) ISBN-13: 978-1478209232

- *Stillness: Images of Wonder, Simplicity, and Depth.* (2012) ISBN-13: 978-1481002233

Made in the USA
Lexington, KY
29 January 2014